RELATIONSHIPS
Don't Have to Suck

9 Happy Couple Hacks that
Keep Relationships Together

*This book is intended for educational and informational purposes only. It is not intended to replace the therapeutic relationship that psychotherapy or even relationship coaching is able to provide.

Contents

Introduction 1

Chapter 1 8

Chapter 2 26

Chapter 3 37

Chapter 4 47

Chapter 5 57

Chapter 6 68

Chapter 7 95

Chapter 8 110

Chapter 9 120

Chapter 10 129

Introduction

There's a large portion of the population that is staying in broken relationships that are clearly not the right fit for them. So much time is wasted with the wrong person that we miss out on the right person. There are so many resources, books, podcasts, workshops, and even couples counseling and/or coaching that is available on this topic. So you're probably wondering if the purpose of this book is just to rehash all of the same material you have already learned—just be kind and send out good juju.

I'm confident my book is unique because it doesn't just advertise how cool it is to be a kind person within the context of a relationship. I think that's great and all, but we have couples with cruddy childhood histories, we have trauma bonds, codependence, high-intensity emotions, grief and loss, and much, much more. To me, that requires a much bigger, more global look at the relationship as a whole. So this book gives you a macro lens rather than focusing on one specific problematic area at a time.

I'm not here to waste your time by trying desperately to sort through one area at a time. I want you to look at your relationship against all the happy couples that I've coached and get BEDAZZLED. Either recognize that your relationship fits nicely into the dance of happy couples, or recognize that you might need to get BEDAZZLED elsewhere. Either way, I'd like to be your guide along the way.

So who is this for?

You're in the right place if you're looking for a partner, currently have a rocky partnership, or you're in the midst of finding some greener pastures. This book is for you if you keep feeling like you're hitting a dead end in terms of landing on a partnership that could be fuel for your soul, literally making you a better human every day. Or feeling frustrated that every day your partnership seems to get a little worse. Or leaving the relationship is bringing you so much angst. Rings a familiar bell? Wanting something to change and actually doing a full workup on why you should stay or go are typically two very different things.

This book is also for you if you have high hopes of designing a partnership that matches other people with seemingly incredible partnerships. I'm certain they have freed up the emotional baggage that comes with a dysfunctional partnership and they are able to put their energy into places that feel significantly more fulfilling. Imagine a relationship that is unconditionally supportive, so you can live your best life while having a lifelong believer in your limitless potential. To me, there's no better life to live.

So who is this dr_meaghan lady anyway?

You might be asking yourself why it makes sense to listen to me. I totally get it. I also struggle with taking others' guidance and direction. I'd much prefer to learn the incredibly hard life lessons on my own, *ha ha*. But the life lesson that I'm about to share with you seemed a little too hard *and* way too flipping long, so my hope is that I can maybe decrease the level of impact that you sustain.

I spent nearly a decade of my young adulthood with a man who just wasn't that into me. Obviously, I knew nothing about what it meant to be with someone who wasn't into me. I think my assumption was that if you're dating and have committed to a serious relationship, then you are certainly into each other. Come to find out that relationships aren't quite that linear and I could have been paying much more attention to subtle warning signs. There were so many warning signs! But in the end, he eventually left me. It wasn't just the loss of the relationship, even though that crushed me, it was also the loss of my entire sense of community. Starting from scratch was a bitch.

So I wallowed in my own self-pity for a hot minute, peeled myself up off the ground, and finished my master's in clinical psychology and my doctorate in organizational leadership. I was on a mission to find a different way of navigating through tricky relationship dynamics. And after being featured in *The Knot*, *Huffington Post*, Bustle, *Men's Health*, *Self Magazine*, Evernote, PureWow, Psych Central, Medical News, *Newsweek*, *New York Post*, Health.com, Refinery29 and Verywell, I decided that the community was probably ready for my global happy couple hacks.

Knowledge is power, right? If we know better, we are responsible for doing better. And I want to reveal all the secrets in terms of how people are getting these partnerships where they can live their best life and still have the most loving space to blossom into who they were meant to be. By following my own hacks, I was able to find that kind of partnership that I envisioned, and I would love nothing more than for you to find something of equal or greater value for yourself.

What you're going to learn

In order to have this partnership of your dreams and therefore become the best version of yourself, we are going to need to be on the same page. Happiness looks a little different for everyone, but to me, it is the ability to be authentically you without very many hurdles impeding that (aka relationship baggage). So chapter 1 dives right into what it means to acknowledge what the best version of yourself looks like—needs, wants, and desires, all conceptualized in a nice pretty package that we can present to the partner of our dreams.

Chapter 2 focuses on communication, which includes all the things related to the presentation of our needs, wants, and desires. I am very interested in both the verbal and nonverbal forms of communication. The communication culture in a relationship feels like it is driving the majority of the other machinery in our journey with another. A well-oiled communication pattern often overflows to other areas of the relationship.

Chapter 3 emphasizes the importance of fighting fair. While we don't necessarily need to agree with our partner, we certainly need to respect them, offer support, and validate their feelings. We need to save space for both partners to have a right to share and feel safe in their share.

Chapter 4 pushes for a voluntary, active involvement in the daily grind. This can look very different depending on the relationship, but sometimes that involves parenting, assisting with pets, doing chores and responsibilities as they come up, and ultimately having some forethought in terms of contribution.

Chapter 5 takes us into the bedroom, where we can explore different variations of keeping the spice alive. This isn't just about sex, it's also about intimacy and love languages, so we can assure our partner that we are bringing safety and security to the table.

Chapter 6 takes a deep dive into how you're economically supporting the relationship. Again, this can look a little different for everyone, but ultimately we need to chip in some cash, some parenting, some volunteering, taking care of a complex set of odds and ends. Something. Anything. Two people investing in a partnership will always be better than one.

Chapter 7 is all about your role in the community. Your relationships with friends, family, coworkers, professionals, groups, clubs, and teams. Being a part of a larger purpose outside of yourself can go a long way. Plus, the skills we learn from people in the community can easily transfer over into the skills that we demonstrate in a relationship.

Chapter 8 is where our sense of self comes into play. It is our self-esteem, our pride and joys, hobbies, passions, and interests. All the things that make us tick and then some. Two whole people coming together to create an addendum to someone's life will always be better than partial people trying to use the relationship to create that wholesomeness for them.

Chapter 9 focuses on our emotional depth. The ability to read a room and perceive that someone might be going through a rough time. Being able to set yourself and your own needs aside to show up for your partner in the way that they need. It is a separation between our own feelings and the feelings of another.

Chapter 10 puts everything together in a quick, easy to understand, objective way. So you can take BEDAZZLED with you from start to finish in your journey to either find the partnership of your dreams, sort through the current one that's making you miserable, or just entirely launch in a brand new direction.

Now that you know where we are headed, let's make this happen for you...

Chapter 1

BECOMING Ourselves is no Easy Feat...

This brings me to the first step in our journey together. **BECOMING**. This step is probably the scariest in a lot of ways. What this step does is start to bring the challenges to light. Because the more we understand ourselves, our needs, our wants, our desires, the more we stop valuing the people that can't align with our vision. While this book is specifically about intimate partnerships, you'll start to notice that it will apply to other people in your life in similar ways. We are the average of the company we keep and therefore our enlightened selves won't be able to carry toxic baggage with us.

But what have you learned about yourself thus far? This understanding can come in the form of life experiences, other people's feedback, your own spiritual work, therapy, books, podcasts, self-help courses, or a variety of different assessments. But if you don't know yourself, we need to figure out who you are. The more we know about you, the better apt we will be to advertise that commitment to yourself to others. If you don't look out for your own needs, I can promise you that nobody will give a f#$% about your needs.

Let's go back to your childhood. How was it? Did you walk away relatively unscathed or do you find yourself stuck in a trauma trench that feels thick and overwhelming? Maybe even somewhere in between. We need to figure out what we are going to do with your childhood. Some people need to fine tune items that they want to take on into their adult life that their childhood didn't offer them. Other people vow never to take any piece of their childhood into their adult life ever again. But I think most the important thing is what side of the fence we are going to be on here. There's no shame in the admission of either side because we are trying to get you to the best possible partnership rather than worry about your family member's opinion of what you should or shouldn't be doing with your childhood.

List the things that you are taking with you from your childhood. Similarly, list the things that you are leaving behind. For me, I wanted to take the abundance of love and all the "you can be anything you want to be." But I wanted to leave behind the financial constraints independent from having a dad who worked and/or traveled so much. While our childhoods don't have to make or break us, we have to consciously pick the things that we want to have in our lives and the things that we want to let go of so we don't find ourselves repeating lifestyles that aren't in alignment with the best version of ourselves.

As important as the decision to take certain items of your childhood with you and leave other items behind is the reflection on how you care for yourself. This is another area that is probably because you have either watched others care for themselves or you have watched others completely self-sacrifice. What I mean by this is watching other people find their purpose, especially the ones closest to you.

The difference between people who have found their purpose and people who have not is actually quite astonishing. People who have found their higher calling tend to leave space for a deeper connection with themselves, a higher level of consciousness that allows them to intertwine moments of self-care, self-love, and ultimately gratitude. Parenting from a position of gratitude and abundance is significantly different from parenting out of basic survival needs. And honestly, toxicity fills the spaces that aren't occupied with passion, purpose, and love relatively quickly.

So what are you doing to carve out space for you? I'm not talking about the pedicures, manicures, massages, drinking with your friends, watching sports, and luxury travel. Those items can definitely be part of this, but I'm talking more about what you're doing to close the gaps between where you dream of being and where you are at this immediate moment. What are you doing to connect with something higher than yourself to fuel yourself? We have to know where we are headed or any road will do and, well, there are some pretty cruddy roads out there. For me, this looks like meditation and/or prayer, depending on what kind of day it has been. Shit days require way more of these things than great days. Why? Because shit days are heavily dependent on the bullshit you feed yourself. So talking yourself out of your own head is quite the battle sometimes.

I also want to talk about your coping skills. Yah, I know, buzzkill. But how we cope with stress is also something that we watch. I saw a stat at one point that said being raised with a primary caregiver who struggled with serious mental illness led to an 80 percent chance of acquiring similar reactions to stress. Obviously nature plays a role in how mental illness develops as well, but being around someone all the time who has the capacity to respond to triggers in a way that feels loud, exaggerated, or even scary at times dramatically influences our own reactions. And guess what? We get to spend a large portion of our adulthood trying to temper the reactions that we were taught. Do any of us get by unscathed? Certainly not. We are all battling demons you know nothing about. You're not alone, so let's buck up and find a way to do better than our caregivers did.

One of my friends shared a story about how, as a child, she would get yelled at, berated, if she spilled something. As a child this was incredibly traumatic for her because she remembers feeling so clumsy. She said that she's still relatively clumsy today. She said that she didn't know this wasn't so great until she spilled milk at her in-laws' house and started crying (as an adult). Her mother-in-law came up to her, tapped her shoulders and said, "Honey, no need to cry over spilled milk." She told me, "That moment in time forever changed my approach with my own kids." Crying over spilled milk *does* feel silly.

So it is important to hold our own childhoods up against other childhoods as an adult. What feels good? What feels bad? It is important to be open to learning other ways because there's a pretty good chance that somebody else somewhere else has a better way of doing things than we do. Never shut down the opportunity to learn and educate yourself about a better way. There are coping styles that can work really well for us: the power of meditation, prayer, a larger sense of community. There are also coping styles that can work against us: an obsession with the gym, numbing through screens, and addiction. But we don't instantly know what this means to us. It's a trial by fire kind of thing, we are all learning as we go.

I am interested in how we incorporate others into our coping skills, styles, and patterns. Do we ask for help? Do we delegate when things hit the fan? Do we recognize when we are drowning and how incredibly helpful a lifeline would be? I'd hate to beat a dead horse here, but if you were raised by a martyr like I was, you will suffer to the greatest of depths to avoid changing the "I'm an independent person" principle. So where does that leave me? I'm terrible at asking for help. My ship needs to sink to the bottom of the ocean before I might have a thought that I should phone a friend. Part of my self-discovery involved sharing that I'm terrible at asking for help from other people in hopes that they would toss me a life preserver even if I tried to convince them I didn't need one. Here's a nice takeaway. People don't help when you need help if you don't tell them all the deets about where, what, when, and how you need help. Nobody is capable of reading your mind.

There are a few things I regularly need when I get stressed. These things I must communicate with others otherwise they would never know. Because I'm an avoidant attachment style (great thing to figure out about yourself, by the way!), I need space to regain my composure. This isn't a casual need for space like a five to ten minutes here and there. This is like a full two- to three-hour reset. Believe me, as a parent of two young children, this is a lot to ask for. I feel guilty every time I ask for it. But the other side of this reset is glorious. I literally feel like a brand new person. I use the time to meditate, feel caught up on work, and to reflect on my vision board—where I see myself in the future and what I am so grateful for in the moment. I don't know if there are people who can do this immediately, amid complete chaos, but my hat goes off to you if you can. I'm like a long-distance runner rather than a sprinter, immediate wind up with the slowest of wind downs.

Something else that I need is for someone to talk me off the ledge. I need someone who can present on the other side of the argument, forcing me to see things through a different lens. This can't be just any person. This has to be a person whom I look up to and respect, someone who already has coping skills intact that are rather impressive. We all need people like this. People whom we idolize because they are put together in a way that allows them to take an illogical grouping of information and transform it into something bite-sized and malleable. Those people exist! But I would argue they are rather rare. No worries if you can't find one right away. We can always offer specific directives to give you several perspectives to choose from. Almost like multiple choices. As long as we have the ability to consider how someone else might view the same situation, we get ourselves off the linear perspective that only our way is the right way. Mental flexibility is a big thing for me because I'm so flipping stubborn, but my husband has managed to crack that code. I'm confident that your dream partner can too (with a little bit of guidance).

The last thing that I need is a longer period of time than others. I need others to give me more grace. Or be able to give myself more grace when others can't offer that to me. I'm incredibly strong-willed and while I work on that a little bit each day, it takes me significantly longer to switch between the here and now and seeing beyond the clouds. What does that mean? In order to work through stress, I have to force myself to understand that this thing I am stressed out about is probably smaller than I would imagine. I need to zoom in to work through the problem, but I need to zoom out to put my problem up against other problems to see if my reaction is congruent. I do this over and over again until the Instant Pot valve is released. I love my Instant Pot and it does great things, but man, it sure does scare the hell out of me. Sorry. I digress.

Those are a few examples of what I need to recover from stress, but what have you found that is most helpful for you? And once again, I'm a little interested in what you need to recover from stress. Long-term, toxic, chronic stress puts so much weight on our body and mind and with that kind of extra baggage, we aren't seeing through the clouds at all. If your physical body is popping up with a whole bunch of things that seem really out of alignment, check your stress levels, get a lab pulled for your cortisol levels. It's a nasty little bugger. The brain and body connection is everything and we only get one opportunity not to completely mess it up.

What you need is equally as important as what drives you nuts. Maybe it's people chewing with their mouths open, or putting their dirty clothes everywhere other than the hamper, or people who have a double standard—asking more from you than they would ask of themselves. Whatever drives you nuts needs to be either something that you create space from or something that you give others a heads-up about. That increases the probability that you and others are mindful of the thing(s) that absolutely drive you bonkers. We don't need to go out of our way to access something that is guaranteed to stimulate an aversive trigger.

If I'm not in the right headspace, you better believe that I'm not all that interested in someone bossing me around. Me perceiving someone as pushing a particular agenda on me, acting as though they know everything, or just trying to get a reaction from me could get an angry reaction. People tend to react in a way that makes them personally absorb the problem as their own, which makes them sad. Or people are riddled in paralysis or fear as a primary disposition. Or some of us, me included, fall into the "just get pissed off and deal with it later" category. I'm less interested in what the disposition is and more interested in what we do with our tendencies. My mantra has become, "letting other people drive an angry reaction is the same as giving them permission to determine my emotional condition." I'm not about to let other people control my emotional condition. Nobody should have that kind of power over us.

There's a pretty strong correlation between people with an avoidant attachment style and having an angry predisposition. Why? Because whether people perceived their childhoods as needing to take care of business on their own in order to survive or they needed to achieve some sort of unrealistic expectation, anger puts up a protective barrier. You don't see the anger come through as much with a secure attachment style because childhoods that have allowed a secure attachment set up a decent dynamic with the outside community. There's less of a need to protect oneself and more of an ability to see others as an additional resource that can help.

I'm not entirely sure why I came out with an avoidant attachment style. My parents were great. My dad passed away within a couple months of this man ditching out on me, and man, that compacted the trauma. He was such a lover, he helped me work through all the hardships in life with unconditional positive regard. The man worked his tail off and was often gone; maybe that left me with some daddy issues. But combining him with my mom equalled hella high expectations. "Shoot for the moon, and land among the stars" kind of thing. My little family of four, all we did was hustle. All three of us are hustlers. We never sit still, always on the go. And I think there's a whole bunch of self-critique that kicks up if we don't have tangible performance metrics. No rest for the weary over here. But! I'm working on it.

Anxious attachment styles often have a component of deep sadness and a fear of the unknown. Anxious attachment styles come from homes that are incredibly inconsistent and often chaotic. Sometimes being able to feel fulfilled, as though basic needs are met. But also being met with a "people are untrustworthy and certainly capable of bad things." It's important to note that attachment styles are fluid—different attachment styles come out for different situations. But I think we all have a predominant attachment style that shows up more regularly than others.

Different attachment styles are typically attracted to each other. It feels pretty common to see couples with both anxious and avoidant tendencies. One member of the partnership is trying to maintain the peace. The other member of the partnership is trying to actively defend themselves or remove themselves from the scene entirely. I'm less interested in what attachment style is carrying over from our childhoods. I'm more interested in how we identify and notify those around us so they can give us a little grace as we awkwardly try to improve it. It can be something as simple as. "Today, I am going to show up with more grace and lean in to help others." Or as complicated as, "I vow to trust people unless they give me very specific evidence of the contrary." Let's work on our tendencies. Always.

We come in with a certain set of needs that are dependent on a complex set of criteria, but so do the people we choose to have as partners. I think I have referenced many times throughout this book that we typically pick people who are very different from us, and the difference in needs seems to stand out in the same way. Different needs are completely fine as long as both parties agree to offer to meet needs in a way that has nothing to do with the way of meeting needs they are most comfortable with. And! That both parties have some capacity to meet their own needs in one way or another, practicing the ability to self-soothe, if you will.

How do we know if our partner is meeting their own needs? Remember when I talked about passion? Well, this is also where this understanding comes in handy. We need partners who are so passionate about something that they can get lost in its regular pursuit. But not so lost in their pursuit of passion that it derails them of the space to give back to any other categories of their life, such as the relationship they have with you. Bonus points if this passion makes them money because today, sole providers have a heck of a hard time supporting an entire household on their own. It makes sense that this particular passion(s) give them some sort of drive that you don't have to provide for them. Dragging someone through life looks like a path that is made for the superheroes in this world. While I have a high drive, it isn't high enough to carry the weight of two people. Plus, people who can meet their own needs can often meet other people's needs, and that's exactly what you're looking for here.

If we have made our needs crystal clear to our partner, can they meet them? I'm not talking about their ability to say that they meet them. A lot of people talk a big talk, but when you see them try to actually put things into action, they chronically fall short. I'm talking about saying that you'd like a hair job (you know, where your partner plays with your hair) and there's a fairly short period of time before they commit to the hair job. Not because they are dying to give you a hair job, but because you don't ask for it 24/7 and they know it is an emotional call on your part. Meeting this need with a sense of urgency guarantees that your partner sees outside of themselves long enough to care for you. All bets are off if you overuse requests. More to come on that.

What is your partner's reaction to your requests to get your needs met? Equally as important as meeting the need is the reaction to the request for the need to be met. I have seen it all: rolling eyes, grunting, moaning, making crude, offensive statements. I am okay with "not right now," but I'm not okay with making a mockery of your asks. Unless, like I said, you're abusing the request and not paying attention to the need for a volley back and forth. Even if you perform the need that your partner asks for after throwing a tantrum, from my experience, you get very little credit for the performance. I am all about positive reinforcement so, if needs are going to be met, it needs to be without such great resistance. We all want some credit around here, right?

Another important reflection is whether you can meet your partner's needs. Some people have outrageous and unrealistic needs. Over the course of my career I think about incredibly lofty sex needs independent from the external pressures of raising a family or running a household, pursuing an aggressive career or trying to go back to school. While sex certainly needs to be on the table, demanding that sexual intensity and frequency stay the same independent from what's going on in the world feels unfair. It also feels unfair that sex doesn't have rights to fluidity in the same way that other categories do. Sex can turn into an addiction just like anything else, and being on the receiving end of someone's addiction feels like a pretty icky place to be.

I had this fear that someone that I love and care for would have gifts as a primary/only love language need. Goodness. I'm the worst gift giver. I try to stay within a certain budget and that most definitely translates into a shitty gift. I've heard that the best gifts are the most thoughtful and least expensive, but I haven't really nailed that art. I try to ask people what they want, but that always feels inauthentic, like a giant cop out. So maybe I'm just not meant to be with partners that *love* gifts. Being up front about my hopeless inability to meet this need has been fairly helpful for me. There's transparency in admitting our faults, or at least that's what I've been told.

But first of all, the needs need to be realistic for the average human to attain. Second, the needs need to be something that is regularly in our wheelhouse. If one partner demands certain needs from their partner, but their partner actually can't achieve those needs for a wide array of reasons, everyone loses. The asking partner loses because they don't get their needs met. The potential giver of the needs loses because they will never get positive reinforcement for a job well done. Talk about a driver of wedges. This is a big enough mismatch to drive a partnership apart.

So we figure out our needs, desires, and wants. We also figure out the thing(s) that drives us nuts. We take some nuggets from our childhood and we leave some behind. We always work on our reactionary disposition. We think about how we are caring for ourselves and keep our burnout at bay. We reflect on our coping skills and assess whether they are positive or negative. And we develop boundaries around the knowledge we have about ourselves so that we can land it on our partners. We can see whether they sink or swim with the expertise that you have about yourself.

And I wanted to add that it is never too late to figure out what we need, what we don't need, and how to present those things to our partner. In fact, I encourage this self-discovery independent from where we are in life. The only caveat here is about partners who have gotten used to not fulfilling your needs or intentionally triggering you or the ones that aren't really interested in growing to be better: there's going to be an incredible amount of resistance in this space. What doesn't kill us only makes us stronger though, right?

A couple ideas to expand on your own self-development:

- Take a few assessments. Myers-Briggs, Enneagram, the Love Language Quiz, DiSC Personality Test (figure out what color you are). All of these assessments will give you a basic understanding of where you stand.

- Take a few career assessments to see where you find the most passion. It's pretty cool to see how your recommended career path lines up with your current career path. Or maybe it doesn't line up at all.

- Develop a regular functional outlet for stress. Meditation, prayer, physical movement, groundedness, a massage, craniosacral, a therapist, a priest. Go for a professional rather than a friend. But a friend is fine if there's no other option.

- Join a team that's a little outside your comfort zone. Not traumatizing. Just outside your comfort zone.

- Plan a trip in the future, access a coach, read a new self-help book, listen to a podcast, go to the mountaintop and scream your face off.

Guess what else happy couples have that the average couple doesn't have?

Happy couples are constantly working on themselves so they can show up as the best version of themselves. But they also have this other amazing attribute...

Chapter 2

EXPRESSION is Everything

Can **EXPRESSION** fix this mismatch of one person's needs and the other person's inability to meet them? My gut impulse is to say no. That no communication can fix mismatches. But then other couples have taught me something very different that pushes me more toward a maybe or even a yes. You know what communication style can work through most things, whatever is put on the table? Let me share the best-case scenario and then I'll take you through what the worst-case scenario looks like. Deal?

The first thing that I am looking for in communication patterns is the ability to validate the concerns of their partner before moving on to anything else. Hear me out when I say that I am not asking partners to agree with each other. That would be silly because typically very different people find each other. What I am asking for is that partners are able to show up in a vulnerable space (sharing anything is a vulnerable space) and be met with interest, acceptance, and validation. If you want more sharing in a partnership and every time a partner shares, it is met with distaste, I promise you that sharing will decrease over time.

I look for people that can validate the whole package—not just the content that is shared, but the feelings that are interwoven within the context. Feelings can be loud, exaggerated, and not even justified. But we can't be shamed for the feeling that pops up or the level of intensity that pops up with it. Shutting down feelings is the equivalent of shutting down our partner's validity as a human being. I wish partners knew how much power they have in terms of either cultivating their partner's self-worth or absolutely destroying it. We don't want to repetitively miss an opportunity to let our partner know that their feelings are valid and that they have a place in our world.

I have no shortage of big feelings. They are completely unjustified, irrational, and really don't demonstrate that I've spent the majority of my adult life figuring out what people need to stabilize themselves. While I deserve to be told that I've lost my mind, although temporarily, my husband doesn't go there. He usually braces himself and goes for a "That makes sense. I hear you." So by validating my feelings, I get to remove some onion layers and reveal what exists behind the rage. Come to find out it's the most timid of little girls leftover from never really fitting in. By acknowledging that it's okay to feel the way I feel, I get to move on to why I could do better in the future.

Closely aligned with validation is this need to take a scrap of ownership. I'm not talking about anything fancy here in terms of taking ownership for the entire thing. I'm saying that by being capable of owning and vowing to commit to behavioral change in the future, we are working toward a culture where both sides drop their defense mechanisms in order to align. Small bouts of ownership go a long way here. For me, I am well-versed in taking ownership for a few recurring themes. I can always own my tone (too intense), or my body language (too defensive), or the lengthy period of time it requires to get over myself in order to align. Having ownership problems and outwardly acknowledging them feels very different than having ownership problems and denying that you have them. The receiving end of a partner that doesn't think they should own anything ever is typically internalization, guilt, and shame, which are all feelings that have an amazing time stacking themselves on top of each other.

So validating our partners and then finding a mutual level of ownership. If we have these two items, we can build the basic part of the foundation. But I want to expand this to include solutions-focused engagement. I have some couples who get completely lost in the weeds and never solve any problems. I have other couples who do a whole lot of solving problems, but completely miss the validation and ownership portion of the expectation. But it is incredibly powerful to come to a conversation with a version of where we would like it to go. If the purpose of any conversation is to create more intimacy and higher levels of alignment, it is significantly easier to design a conversation to get there. If the purpose is to feel out who is more right, well, any path of chaos will get there. I like competition in terms of who can think of the most creative idea to solve some problems, even if the solution to a problem is to support more and fix less.

The older I get the more I realize that I have very little tolerance for conversations that go nowhere. I have so little time! I feel like I need to guard my time wisely in order to stay on top of all the things I want to accomplish in such a short period of time. And honestly, once we start this pattern of "We aren't here to make our lives better. We are here to fight," it is incredibly challenging to dig ourselves out of that trench. A certain culture has been created and I have run into many people who actually don't have any interest in doing anything better than chronically fighting. I don't want to let it slip past us that fighting is incredibly exciting and for those partners who have been raised in chaos, fighting can easily be normalized.

Just like fighting can be normalized, so can an optimistic or pessimistic attitude.

Optimism and pessimism—either theme can be normalized in family cultures. Not to be on extreme ends of the pendulum so much, but sometimes extremes help us conceptualize what the gray area looks like. But people can be largely optimistic about most things. Obviously they will have the occasional slip up when life really starts to stack the lemons, but you can more generally count on them to give positive spins when life smacks them in the face. Because they have the ability to put positive twists on their own way of thinking, they also have a tendency to do that for others. Reaping the benefits from someone who talks about how the rainbow is just about ready to come from the storm can be exhilarating. It is incredibly helpful to be in the throes of a deeper discussion and one partner is able to see our positive intentions, or the secret positive hidden message rather than take us literally by how we are presenting ourselves in the moment. I think of toxic positivity as not being helpful at all. It feels fake and manufactured. It also has the ability to make people feel guilty for feeling anything less than incredibly happy. That's not what we are going for either.

But pessimism can destroy a partnership. Chronically looking at life as half empty pushes the other partner to fill in the gaps. Constantly trying to defend themselves against the negativity. Constantly justifying why it makes sense to keep fighting. Constantly carrying both partners through the thick and the thin, buying time before they combust at the seams. Teaching someone the art of choosing happiness is only effective if it lands on willing ears. Trying to talk someone into a certain perspective before they are willing will absolutely defeat you. Plus, I don't think it is our job as a partner to argue with someone about whether or not we choose happiness within the context of a relationship. You either want it or you don't.

Now, I don't want to say that we should just write off pessimistic partners, because there are those occasional cases where partners have been largely optimistic at one time, got slapped in the face a few times, became pessimistic, and are now avidly working toward the light. But choosing pessimism because you can should alter your spidey senses a little bit.

Choosing pessimism typically has an emotionally unstable link in there as well that we need to be made aware of. People who live pessimistically are also searching for evidence that confirms their perspective. My logic is that if you look hard enough for something, you will most certainly find it. Finding evidence to prove that you, other people, and the world suck brings a lot of negative feelings with it. Whatever we think about is what we fuel emotionally.

Thinking negatively and feeling negatively often have a rock bottom in there somewhere. What goes down must come up in terms of feeling really low, which oftentimes can bring a random wave of exhilaration. Riding this wave with a partner can lead to anxiety because we never know how long one particular phase is going to last and what the levels of intensity will be. Again, emotional instability is something we can work with if the partner is interested in exploring, acknowledging, and working through it. But without the commitment to do better here, riding an emotional wave that you didn't create feels unfair. I can think of so many couples where one partner is forced to ride the waves of another and the outcome is feeling regularly defeated.

Pessimism has the ability to impact people's view of themselves, others, and the world. It feels so pervasive in so many ways. When pessimistic people describe themselves, they typically undercut their own value. Even if other people offer direct, positive feedback, the pessimist still sees a comeback that dismisses it. Remember when I said there's a search for evidence that confirms their pre-existing belief structure? Well, positive feedback doesn't do that. Nor does a largely positive belief in their worth. Not only do they look at themselves from a negative lens, but other people get blanket statements of untrustworthiness, inauthenticity, and disingenuousness. They keep their distance from people. And the world is falling apart. Gripes about politics, religion, or other generally useless material flies out of their mouth on the regular. We can spend our lives talking someone into being positive or we can hope they make their own call to do better and move on until we see actual proof.

That leads me to a conversation about the type of conversations I would hope for in a relationship. I think about those painfully awkward first dates that we go on. I'm constantly coaching people to keep a lookout for someone's ability to volley. We need to learn how to volley a conversation and the person on the receiving end also needs to learn how to volley. I think we are responsible for learning those skills because odds are that it hasn't come naturally to anyone on the planet. So what do I mean by volleying a conversation? I mean that we can both ask questions and give answers, without dominating any particular category. Sometimes people get nervous, and what we see with nervousness is more of a programming effect kick in. Getting stuck on one particular category because they are scared that changing their role in the conversation makes them lose all conversational ability entirely. Usually this wears off so I'm not particularly concerned about this.

What I'm worried about is a dominance with talking that leaves very little room for our partners or our potential partners to kick in. There's something about wanting all the attention, admiration, or control that doesn't sit well with me because the farther we go on the end of the scale that is dominating, the more we hush our partner, and oftentimes, that can be rather predictive in terms of where we are headed with other behaviors as well. Our partners need to be curious about our lives. Always. They need to be interested in how we tick, what fuels our soul, and what our biggest fears are. They need to be able to hear about complete blasphemy and come back with a simple, "Wow, that sounds really frustrating. What can I do to help?" Even if they agree with us not at all.

Our feelings matter significantly more than what our feelings are about. Read that again. A lot of partnerships get lost in the weeds with your feelings only mattering if there was something legitimate to spark the feeling. But my argument against that is that feelings are subjective, so who are we to say that someone shouldn't feel a certain way because we wouldn't feel that same thing if that thing happened to us? In our communication styles it is great to make feelings a priority, but if you can't make feelings a priority, you have to leave some space for them. "I can see how you feel a certain way" goes a long way here. Even cooler if we can have conversations about both parties having very different feelings over the same incident and then validating both of the feelings. Because we seek out intimate partnerships to feel validated, right? It is our person that we want to spend forever with, so hopefully they are our biggest cheerleader for all the things: hopes, dreams, failures, and feelings. Hopefully they are talking to you about you enough to where they push you to keep fighting for something that feels so out of reach.

So everyday communication about neutral topics has some requirements. We should look for people's ability to align, their ability to take ownership for anything, their ability to save space for big feelings, having a positive attitude, and their ability to take turns. But even though conversational ability carries a lot of weight, I want to emphasize that *how* we engage in conflictual conversation is everything.

And it's never too late to change how we **EXPRESS** ourselves. We can always choose to focus on positivity. We can always choose to work on tempering loud, explosive feelings. We can stop interrupting and start listening. We can choose to get really enthusiastic when our partners reach out to us with their emotional calls. It is harder to change the older we get, but I've seen some pretty miraculous changes from people who were never expected to change.

So how we express ourselves sets the stage really nicely for our next topic.

Forms of **EXPRESSION** that I love:

- ➢ Flooding our partners with gratitude every day. Why are we grateful they chose us?

- ➢ Listening with only the intention of reflecting on what they share and giving a quick summarization.

- ➢ Nobody likes people who interrupt them. Come up with a cue for interruption that both of you can reinforce.

- ➢ You can cuss, but I don't know a single happy couple that cusses at each other.

- ➢ Practice groundedness together: 5 things you can see, 4 things you can touch, 3 things you can hear, 2 things you can smell, and 1 thing you can taste. Repeat until emotional regulation kicks into gear.

Chapter 3

Be DELICATE with Conflict

I always joke with my clients that I never travel with a friend who I haven't stormed with. Because you know that as soon as you travel together and you're in the same space for longer periods of time, that's when the storm will occur. It's awkward in public settings especially if you have to end the trip early and bail on future reservations. My reasoning behind this is that everyone has a different way of storming. Some people storm within relatively average limits. They are **DELICATE** when they storm. Other people storm and blow people out of the water. When I think about storming within relatively average limits, I think about slightly heated tones, distorted facial expressions, and emotional dysregulation that makes it difficult for either party to absorb new material or see their partner's side.

The other kind of storming involves intimidation, threats, and derogatory comments. Somebody is out to be a winner and nothing will get in their way. People walk away from a storm like this absolutely destroyed. It looks like that scene in *The Hangover* where they end up on the roof and have no idea how they got there. People walk away with no self-esteem, fear of the unknown, hopelessness, and a whole bunch of questions about whether this is the right fit for them. Every. Single. Time. It takes days or even weeks to recover and it often leaves behind a nasty taste in your mouth even after the fight has come to a close. Why? Because we aren't fighting to solve problems. We are fighting to see who can drudge up the deepest dark past and throw it in their partner's face in the most intense possible way.

I can often tell whether someone is here to solve problems or is here to create them, and I think it has something to do with loyalty. When I see people show up time and time again with helpful, creative ideas, or with a key choice phrase that is able to neutralize the level of emotional content that is going on, it makes me think that they are able to see the relationship for the long haul. It feels like they can go global and they can also get mindful in the here and now, and that feels exhilarating.

There's a certain structure to showing up for a plan that these other groups of partnerships don't necessarily have.

Nobody wants a partnership that isn't going to stay intact. But at the same time, it is harder to see the day-to-day in terms of how they apply or don't apply to a longer term picture. The opposite of loyalty to me is a "winging it" mentality. It is showing up all the time without any sort of clue as to what the future holds and without any sort of clue as to how the current behaviors will dictate the course. It tells me that new material from our partners isn't coming in anymore. In order to be loyal and have a solutions-focused approach, it feels imperative that we are paying attention to our partner, understanding what their needs are, understanding what they don't like, and constantly striving to make those movements because relationships and our partners are fluid.

From my experience, there seems to be a correlation between partners that know for sure their relationship is going to be intact in the future (unless, of course, something catastrophic happens) and higher levels of happiness. When we think about Maslow's Hierarchy of Needs, we have to consider that a relationship staying intact or at least having the confidence to support it staying intact has an easier time getting out of the lowest tier—the safety and security tier. People who feel safe can start to branch out into other important categories like belongingness or self-esteem, and those tiers feel like the most ideal place to be.

That brings me to what happens when there's rigidity in the partnership that prevents an ability to see our partner's life from their particular lens. Maybe it comes in the form of always thinking you're right or you have the best way. I see a lot of professionals who already have a slight undertone of "things are better when they're my way", but then they go to their job and get positively reinforced for the fact that their way has actually turned out something that is positively beneficial. Going home to apply the same "my way or the highway" is unhelpful because our partners could very well have a better way in other categories unfamiliar to us, and humility is what brings the emotional connection. People go where they get positively reinforced, so it makes sense to me that people can get more positive reinforcement in their jobs than they do at home. So making that transition from job to home is going to be especially challenging.

Healthy partnerships will have a different way of communicating at work from the way that they communicate at home. It is this ability to recognize that at work, a lot of times, people are in a position of power or they are involved in a hierarchical structure that is authoritarian rather than authoritative. Coming home to demands of collaboration can feel overwhelming and out of alignment. But at the same time, we are responsible for developing a healthy transition so we can show up in that space with a mentality that respects and values our partners. I want both partners to encourage the transition to be a little bit more malleable when we transition into the home space, so we can show up with a little bit more dedication to equality and viewing our partners as equal players in the game.

I would caution people against showing up in the wrong headspace, especially at home. While I don't think we can get a Get Out of Jail Free card multiple times a day, showing up in the right headspace allows us to respond to someone's emotional content without letting our own seep through the cracks. It is too much to manage two very different people's set of emotions, especially if they are heightened. Gaslighting comes into this space relatively easily when we are completely overwhelmed. Instead of looking at our partner's critique about some portion of our behavior as feedback that we can trust, we look at it as a personal attack. We blow up, have a loud reaction, and then we get labeled as some kind of freak. It is no longer about the slight alteration in the behavior, it becomes about how the reaction has been able to drown out all things conversationally. I want everyone to be taken seriously, for everyone to get a fair chance, and that requires that we don't deplete the validity of the conversation because we have deemed the reaction as too much.

I wanted to save a separate section of my book for rage because it is just that common. If I could pick out the most problematic response to any kind of conflictual conversation, this is where my mind goes. I remember raging at my ex more and more frequently. It was like the more it happened, the more I had the power to shut everything down and/or get this man to grovel. And that felt good. Considering I had no actual control over whether or not he stayed, I liked having a little bit of reprieve. But even though I was getting positively reinforced for bad behavior, I was creating a culture of fear. I think it was well known at that point in my life that I was a wild card and that anything could set me off. I was fragile like a bomb. So was he staying because he wanted to or was he staying because he didn't know the depths of what I could pull off? (Honestly I didn't know that answer either.)

I have a friend whose partner tends to fly off the handle and actually leaves the scene if constructive feedback lands his way. So the positive reinforcement for him is that he doesn't actually have to work through hard things. I'm not convinced that there's any sort of positive reinforcement for her other than finally being able to expel things off her chest that have been building up for quite some time. But over time, this routine has led to a culture where bad things happen and they continue to brush them off for another day that never actually arrives. I'm not sure that it is a culture of fear as much as it is a culture of "I don't share in this space." And having your partner as the one person that you can't go to with hard things is pretty crappy.

In my opinion, if our partners are scared of us or have completely shut down, we have completely lost the battle. A culture of fear that is driven by rage, intimidation, or threats toward aggression has the capacity to completely shut people down. Until people feel safe or heard, they are no longer capable of higher levels of growth. I'm sorry that this is going to come across so bluntly, but a culture of fear is never going to be good enough. There's no rationalization or justification in the world that is going to overcome the degradation that people experience when they are living in fear. If you or someone you know is living like this, my hope is that people keep flooding them with the resources to know better and therefore do better. I completely get it, there are family structures that we don't want to break, and religious values that keep us stuck, and financial unknowns, and societal judgment. But there's nothing worse than sacrificing your soul to a chronic, toxic state of fear.

So conflict can be **DELICATE**, where even though we don't agree with our partner, we certainly respect them. We have mental flexibility and we treat them as though they will be along in the journey for the rest of our lives (even though nobody can predict the outcome here). We are interested in creating a culture where each person can be uniquely them while also building a path to include both partners' perspectives. It's not a perfect agreement as much as it is about making your partner feel safe and ultimately listening way more than you plan on defending yourself. Which brings me to another topic that can cause so many problems in relationships.

Trying to change someone's disposition is a bit more challenging. I haven't seen a whole bunch of success with making a rager stop raging. The same can probably be said about those who internalize conflict and feel really down on themselves. Or people who worry about everything will probably continue on that trajectory. But the good news is that we can always learn how to channel the funk of our disposition in a new way. Maybe we go down in the basement and scream it out. Sometimes I go out in the garage and hoot, holler, and carry on. It's the only spot that my kids hate to be and it is guaranteed they won't follow me. We could go for a run. We could take a hot shower. Maybe we come up with a mantra that says conflict can be 50/50 (or nobody's fault at all). Maybe we unload our worries and deepest fears on a therapist or phone a nonjudgmental friend. There's a way to direct our reactions somewhere other than landing them right on our partner.

Ways to encourage more **DELICACY:**

- ➢ Imagine that you are talking to your supervisor when you are talking to your partner. Would you talk to them the way you are talking to your partner?

- ➢ Have you tried texting an "ouch" when you feel something aversive? Then give a feeling rating. Also give your role in why you may have gotten to the point of feeling that way (short and sweet here). This allows us to take the nonverbals out of the equation.

- ➢ People write better than they talk. Just remember that if you need a lifeline.

- ➢ People who rage need space to rage without being around you. Put a timer on it. The rager and the recipient need to get grounded when they are taking a break. Notice five blue items in the environment around you. Focus on your breath. Get a fidget toy.

- ➢ Choose safety first. Solutions are second.

*Physical abuse, mental abuse, emotional abuse, and sexual abuse should never be accepted. While different people define these concepts in different ways, you need to have a line in the sand that, if crossed, will be reported to people who can help. Here's the Domestic Violence Hotline (they can help you sort through the significance of your experience): 800-799-7233 and depending on the severity, you can always call the emergency or non-emergency number of your local law enforcement.

Happy couples work really hard on communication, especially when they are talking about deeper rooted issues. But not only do they work on their words. They also work on their actions. Which brings us to the next chapter.

Chapter 4

Happy Couples are ACTIVE

Household chores and responsibilities seem to be directly correlated, but at the minimum indirectly correlated. This is our level of **ACTIVITY** in the home. I wish I got a dollar for every time somebody complained about the lack of sex and the other partner complained about the lack of help around the house. We have all heard about this, right? Well, it feels pretty real and relevant to me because when sex is a dominant value to someone, it's really dominant. So dominant, in fact, that it floods out other categories that probably should have some stakes in the game too. Should we *love* household chores and responsibilities? No. Should we treat household chores and responsibilities as a necessary evil? Absolutely. Think about them like the master of all Get Out of Jail Free cards. It might not be that you get immediate gratification for its completion. But I can promise you they are like 401ks in that we can store them up and see the benefit continue to grow. It's an investment in ourselves. It's also an investment in our partnerships.

Guess what some people never ever have a conscious thought about and other people have it on their brains constantly? I could make some gender stereotypes here, but I'll let you connect the dots.

Household chores and responsibilities. While some people are organically more clean than others, I don't know that it correlates directly with household chores and responsibilities. Because being clean doesn't necessarily get the dog fed or get the kids ready for school. For me and many of my comrades, a clean, tidy, organized home is a reflection of my headspace. I can actually talk myself off the ledge by cleaning. It gives me a certain degree of control over my life; even if it's a false sense of control, it does the trick. People who believe that they can influence the condition of their lives are happier than those who feel like we are always the victim of circumstances. So if there's a bad headspace, I turn up the music and get to work. So we can nail the cleanliness of our home, really value that quality, but also forget about the art of contributing in a way that directly helps our partner with the overwhelm of life.

My husband jokes that I have my own furniture moving company. Every time he comes back from a trip, the furniture has been completely rearranged. He's yet to get me on video moving a whole couch down several flights of stairs, but I'm sure he would love nothing more. I'm also relatively curious about what skillset I use to make it happen. Once again though, I can absolutely control the placement of my furniture and if I move it, I have a chance to deep clean in the less obvious spaces. Which are actually disgusting, by the way. Dogs and kid remnants clog up my pet vac every time I do it. But I could probably walk by the dog poop in the yard 50,000 times before picking it up, or forget about the laundry for weeks on end.

My husband must have a standard of cleanliness, but I haven't seen it before. He said it was only activated when he lived with a dirty roommate, which cracks me up. He's quick to jump on the tasks that are in front of his face, like the dishwasher needing to be unloaded or the ten loads of laundry that I haven't given one f#$% about since he's been gone. If he doesn't have a standard of cleanliness and I'm cleaning all the time, we've missed each other. If he's unloading the dishwasher and doing laundry, I feel like I've literally landed on a saint of a hubby.

So how do we connect such different value structures? Well, similar to communicating exactly what we need from our individual reflections we talked about earlier, I encourage couples to communicate exactly what they need in a household. I get some negative feedback from different couples about this because they say that "their partners should just know what to do" or telling their partners what they need somehow signifies them being in a parental role. But here's how I want to pitch this. I know very few people who have actually demonstrated evidence of how powerful their ESP is, so that tells me that people can't largely read anyone else's mind. The couples who are just winging it without really communicating much at all might not feel like a parent, but there's no chance that they feel fulfilled.

So I'm a huge pusher for delegation. On the regular, items go on my Google calendar, the calendar is shared with my husband, then we have our powwow about things that we've noticed on our shared calendars. It feels like a meeting of the minds because we are not only dividing up tasks according to who has preferences, but we are also equally sharing the workload, *and* we are also planning for the future (which is incredibly good for people with avoidant attachment styles). Guilty as charged. After all, you have to try to lock down those avoidant attachment folks.

So this is the first push for the things that I need help with. The first push feels like a rough draft, so there are probably some bugs to fix after the first push. There's wiggle room to trade things back to the original partner, do a different duty that you would prefer more, or add additional tasks at the last minute. But I like to intentionally separate the items that have all week to complete from the items that need to be completed ASAP. Why? Because there are some chores that require a well-defined sense of urgency and honestly, the partner on the receiving end only gets credit for the task if they do the thing immediately.

Let me offer some examples here because I really want to make this sense of urgency a big deal. Saying that we need to get the dog groomed this week is very different from saying that I have Christmas decorations that I just took down and they are in the way until you help me put them in the attic. The dog grooming is variable because we haven't nailed down the date. The Christmas decorations are blocking traffic right now and that will remain a ticking time bomb in someone's mind until it is resolved.

I hear all the things in response to this sense of urgency. I hear that it feels controlling, too intense, bossy, nag-like, and the best one is the nonverbal one—the grunt and the eyeroll regularly crack me up. Sometimes I think an incredibly aversive reaction to being asked to do things that also benefit you creates the parent-child vibe. But instead, having a get-to-it attitude is often met with an abundance of positive reinforcement and gratitude. I don't know about you, but I'm happy to give all the appreciation in the world to someone who takes my need to solve a problem quickly very seriously. Things getting done quickly makes me feel like I'm a priority in my partner's world.

Some people have parents who have waited on them hand and foot. While I think that's great in some ways because a lot of people offer love through acts of service, I also think it can be incredibly disabling for the receiver of it. Some people joke that we marry our parents. I have seen firsthand proof of the reality behind that theory. The opposite sex parent either registers a certain set of characteristics that resonates effectively with the child or the opposite sex parent is entirely repulsive. But those who have had an opposite sex parent who puts them on a pedestal, never allowing them to experience the everyday grunt work that nobody actually wants to do, have a really high predisposition of finding a like-minded spouse.

I think there's more gender equality in the domestic operation of the household. I think it is a really good thing because, like I said, sex and household chores seem to be connected intimately, and if both parties are motivated by one or both of these things, we can set up a pretty sweet gig romantically. Seeing both partners take pride in making their partner's lives easier is a beautiful thing.

I gave this presentation about relationships at one point, and after I was done I opened it up for a Q&A. I remember one of the women in the audience saying that my presentation was great and all about delegating household chores and responsibilities, but there was a zero percent chance that her husband would comply. What I was thinking to myself was obviously different than how I responded, but I remember walking away wondering how women were working with a zero percent compliance rate. Ugh. Do these partners come from parents who never demanded anything from them, have their partners stopped asking for help and therefore created a monster, or a combo of both? But just like the non-negotiable things that we need, doing no household chores and responsibilities isn't an option. Because the lack of the division of labor leads to a multitude of relationship-ending scenarios, I do feel like it is worthy of an ultimatum. "Help me or we need to do some serious reflection on whether we should continue this."

Even from a distance, we can't take the easy road. I know couples that Uber Eats each other when they've had a long day. Or give "thinking of you" kind of flowers. Or an intimate card with a particular fragrance attached to it. Booking a cleaning person or someone to come in and fold your never-ending supply of laundry goes a long way. I love the combo of reserving some FaceTime interactions (quality time) and thinking ahead of the game. Hiring a maintenance person, checking the mail, arranging meals, anything that relieves some degree of the load from our partners.

I think people are scared of rejection more than death. So I would imagine that part of this fear is that demanding what we need help with from our partner will somehow cause them to reject us. While there must be some truth to that, I think the reverse can also be true. Continue to leave all the household chores and responsibilities to me, and I have no choice but to leave you. We have a lot to lose if we continue to self-sacrifice, all the while living without the development of a smooth system.

So you're probably wondering what kind of movement we can have in this space if the train has already derailed. I'm pretty optimistic about making headway here. This may sound a little strange, but sometimes our partners need to see what's in it for them if they were to start contributing in the way that they should. Like a teaser. Maybe it resembles something like a chore chart (for adults, obviously) where the prize is sex, or alone time, or a weekend getaway with your friends. Or some people do better with consequences. I'm a consequence-driven kind of lady so I feel like I can relate to this. "If this particular chore isn't done by the time I get home today, I think we need to do some serious talking about how there's someone better for me than your lazy ass." Just kidding about the latter part. You get the idea. Conveying a strong boundary without being mean about it.

We are trying to develop a system here, a smooth running machine that doesn't require constant communication about it. It is like brushing our teeth, for most of us, we don't think about whether we should brush our teeth. We just do it everyday. There's so much positive reinforcement available in a space where both parties understand that their individual contributions go a long way for the benefit of the relationship.

More ideas to consider:

- ➤ If there are chores that one partner likes more than the other, please give that chore to them.

- ➤ The more things that we can put on a regular rotation, the better. (For example, trash day is the same every week).

- ➤ As often as you can, ask that both of you participate in a chore together. "Hey, I'm happy to fold the laundry if you put it away."

- ➤ Talk about couples that you idolize often. "Did you know that Amy cuts her kids' meat and cheeses into fun shapes? What a rockstar she is."

- ➤ Talk about something major you would like to accomplish together in the future, so there's more buy-in for the little steps along the way.

What seems to be the end result to a contributory partner?

Chapter 5

ZESTFULLY Radiant

Honestly, I didn't really know about this correlation between household chores and responsibility and sex (**ZESTFULNESS**) until I kept seeing it come through with my couples time and time again. In my own marriage I think that sex is a given, not really even something I give much thought to, because my husband helps out anytime the opportunity presents itself. I'm sure he doesn't give much thought to whether or not he should help out. So to me, that feels like a reasonable give-and-take, and there's so much love in that space.

The problem is that relationships can't survive without sex itself or variations of sex (more to come for long-distance couples). But sex has two parts. The first part of sex is the emotional and intimate connection. This seems to be a predominantly feminine characteristic where there's some degree of a tally in their head. A checklist that flows through all of the love languages, not even just the love language that resonates most closely with them. Right? I feel like I'm talking about myself right now. Let's be real. I want to know what household chores were delegated and completed, I want to know whether I've been touched (given a clue about their interest in me), did they think about me for special events (anniversary, birthday, and holidays), have I been on a date in a hot minute, and have they told me how hot I am. LOL. This may seem to be quite an overwhelming inventory, but at the same time I promise to always commit to sex with this very specific list being on the table. I have received feedback that I'm not a dead fish, so that also feels promising.

The second part of sex is the sexual release, the physical gratification. In other words, what is the quality of the sexual experience? Like I said before, a culture of fear can dismantle the sexual experience altogether, and I have plenty of grace to offer people in that particular position. But I have less grace to give without the culture of fear and the sex life is just terrible. I think we have an obligation to explore all the different avenues to create a new spark or a first spark or something that is worthy of talking our partners into. Like I said, that feminine energy is a total bitch sometimes because we are constantly trying to get out of our mental funk, and if the sex is *bad* after we've spent so much time and energy negotiating with ourselves, I just feel like that is the end of our world as we know it.

Most women can orgasm on their own with some sort of vibrating assistance. I have come across so many women who can't orgasm during sex. I often think to myself, what is happening here? You know how to cum, but you aren't transferring that knowledge and skill over to actual sex? Why? I have had a variety of answers here, but the general gist seems to be fear of not accomplishing the orgasm in front of someone else, they don't want to teach their partner the only way that works, or the vibrator is so much better (I *love* this one). So there's some fear of rejection wrapped up in this, but there's also a comparison of the vibration to the real act.

Let's work through the fear of rejection, because who cares if someone judges you when you're having the best time of your life. And why can't we merge vibration with actual sex? You know there are toys for that, right? I think I'm less concerned with hoo-ha size, or breast size, or any other piece of anatomy, and I'm way more interested in whether someone is interested in learning new tricks. I think that characteristic, a willingness to learn, is a fairly valuable trait across the board.

I do have quite a few couples who regularly have had bad sex and nobody is talking about it. If you were raised in an environment that treated sex as taboo, you have a pretty high probability of never sharing how you really feel about the experience with your partner. But the conversation itself, because both partners are interested in sharing, can be one of the most intimate experiences of everyone's lives. There's no possible way that our partners can assume what we need sexually. Even when we feel like the moans, grunts, or gestures are answering those questions, there's nothing quite like the "Hey, when you put pressure on my sacrum the way you did, the orgasm was significantly more intense." Or "Hey, if we could skip the foreplay and get right to the sex, that would be awesome. I'm not in the right headspace for a long sesh tonight." The more clear and the more specific, the better. Sound familiar? Yep! It's just like presenting our needs or delegating household chores and responsibilities.

Defensiveness about sex isn't great, but it's certainly a pretty frequent occurrence. I do think most of the problem is the delivery, but some people are predisposed to defensiveness about sexual feedback independent from how graceful the delivery is. Remember when I talked about how scary rejection is? Well sexual rejection is next level. I totally get why the defensiveness kicks up here. Thinking about the ultimate delivery, I think about the good ole shit sandwich statement. "Hey, sex was kickass. Next time, I want to repeat everything we did tonight, but I'd like to skip the nipple caressing. I think that fix would actually perfect the experience." Anytime we can skip giving feedback in the moment (during the sexual act), the better. Why? Because men who struggle with erectile dysfunction are bound to regress with pointed feedback. And sex should be reserved for the highest level of intimacy and minimal to no amounts of feedback. Just not the right time.

Even worse than getting defensive about any potentially negative sexual feedback is constantly rejecting sexual outreaches. I'll never understand how people just say, "Yah, no sex ever again." Or reject their partner every single time, so they eventually get the message and completely resign to a sexless relationship. To me, no sex isn't ever going to be the right answer. There are very few acceptable reasons for this, but just to name a few: acute trauma, hospitalizations, persistent and/or chronic health issues, acute grief and loss, anything that says you physically *can't* make it happen. But to just say no because you can? I'm not a huge fan. Here's why. I'm pretty sure there's an undertone in any partnership agreement that says, "I promise to try my very best, always." Who our partner fell head over heels in love with needs to be the person we keep trying hard to show up as. Whether it is a particular value structure, a certain sexual rhythm, or a unique set of beliefs. I think there's always going to be room to improve all of these things, but regressions are a much harder sell. Regressing to zero forever is unacceptable.

Anytime we leave our relationships with cracks in the armor, we can't get upset when something negative seeps into those spaces. Cheating, addiction (porn especially, but gambling too), substance abuse, and lying are big things. All of these things creep up before we have a chance to correct our behaviors that may have exacerbated the cracks. Granted, these things can happen without flat-out rejecting our partner's sexual outreaches because if people want to do bad things, there's nothing really stopping them. Partners can't control their partners. But why dramatically increase the odds?

I know a couple different couples from the boomer generation who only had sex to procreate and then never had sex again. But these examples feel unique because both parties went into the unsaid contract with a "we definitely have to have sex to have kids", but at the same time, there's a chance that they both committed to no sex because it was too overwhelming for both. But notice how I referenced that having no sex at all was an agreed-upon decision? I think a contract can change if both parties are on board, but I can't get on board with changing the contract because we feel like it. The deal that we made at the beginning should be part of our priority list as we make our way into a longer term dynamic.

I have noticed that couples do best with an every third day rhythm. Like I've said, there are some variations in here— periods, grief and loss, trauma, relationship-induced fear, health problems. But just like anything else in our life that turns out to be successful, we nurture it a little bit every day or at least on a rhythm that feels more procedural than anything else. Just like we brush our teeth to stay away from halitosis, the dentist, or teeth that fall out of our head. We have sex regularly to keep the train on the tracks. Some people recharge from the physical release and other people recharge through the emotional connection, so depending on how it is set up, it could be mutually beneficial for everyone. This is the *only* thing that we can do to gratify both partners at the exact same moment in time.

There's one caveat about sex on a regular rhythm. I have seen a few cases where sex is used as a tool for secondary gain or manipulation. Having sex on a regular rhythm keeps the questions about lack of interest from their partners at bay, so they can essentially do what feels self-serving. Or having regular sex keeps a family structure intact whereas one of the partners could have been potentially thrown out on the streets without any resources. it's pretty cruddy for our sense of self to sacrifice our bodies for secondary gain. But every time I hear about this, it makes my spidey senses go up, and I can't help but wonder if there's some narcissism or a lot of narcissism underlying this tendency. I usually hear about this when an individual has a chance to pull me away from the couple dynamic, so unfortunately it's not something I can share with the other partner. I'm forced to hold onto a giant dirty secret. Talk about making it incredibly challenging to align with a client.

One more variation of sex that I feel is talkworthy. Like I've said before, major role changes and/or value changes rock a relationship to the core. When it comes to sexuality, I think about monogamy and I also think about open relationships. When we walk into a monogamous relationship, commit to a monogamous relationship, and later realize we'd prefer an open relationship, we can't expect our partner to accept that. That's such a major detour from the original contract to trump their partner's impulsive need to satiate a reckless variation. I've also seen couples who found each other through a kink dynamic and later settled into a groove that seemed more sexually averse than anything else. That seems like a giant value shift that doesn't typically sustain itself. We can't advertise ourselves as being part of a certain group, our partner falls in love with that particular version, we change the version they fell in love with, and we are still expecting them to be happy about the change and hang around.

Long-distance couples have the same obligation. To keep the fire burning from a distance. We shouldn't hold back on sexting, nudes, or live feeds of sexual gratification. While it sucks that both partners can't be there in real life to support each other's needs, we can certainly make up for it with all the technologically advanced means of conveying the same message. Don't be scared. I think we've normalized sexual exchanges a little bit more. Obviously not recommended for teens because of tarnished reputations and such and maybe even consent being an issue. But for the oldie but goodies, why not? Leave out your face if you're really nervous about it. The amount of couples that I've talked into dirty texting each other is quite impressive and it always leads to more **ZEST.**

So sex used in the right way, with both intimacy and physical gratification on the table, can keep the partnership engine well-oiled and on track. Zero isn't the answer. So something between nothing and mind-blowing is the goal. Sex is an excellent metric to let us know how our relationship is doing because it lets us know what each partner is feeling. Feminine energy feels fulfilled through intimacy. Masculine energy feels fulfilled through physical gratification. Sex lets us know that both partners are #winning.

What do we do about no sex? Well, that answer varies. Can I get it to come back? Yes. Can I get it to come back when there's a heavy hitter block? Not as well. A heavy hitter block is the result of feeling unsafe, driven by fear, a trauma history, a medical problem, someone stepped out of the relationship, addiction gets in the way, a disability, etc. If you've made the decision to stop having sex with no heavy hitter, let's find more things that create space for sex. Quality time, hair jobs, massages, nonsexual physical touch. Let's get away from our kids. They are huge buzzkills for couples needing to have regular sex. If there are heavy hitters blocking things: consult with a doc, sign up for a group that is also struggling with similar things, listen to sexual self-help books, or link with a therapist. We need to work on ourselves before we can get involved with a healthy partnership. If the relationship is driving the heavy hitter, use minimal-cost apps like Lasting, or do a free couples challenge, or find a group that has a whole bunch of struggling couples who help each other. Cost-effective methods can be just as effective as relationship coaching.

Here are some ideas for bringing back the **ZEST:**

> - Put sex on a schedule. Sync with other cool things like date night or chill Sunday afternoons or Friday nights.
>
> - Or don't put sex on a schedule, but have a three-day window where you need to make something happen within that time.
>
> - Bring something kinky into the dynamic. Something that makes you feel a little uncomfortable, but also not unsafe.
>
> - Have a nonsexual physical touch space where you could cuddle, hold hands, or rub each other's shoulders. Give time for the flower to bloom, especially if we are working with a dead bud.
>
> - Reflect on the quantity and intensity of intimacy because sex typically follows the same trajectory.
>
> - Learn how to cum in the best way so you verbalize that to your partner.

So there's a direct correlation between sex and household chores and responsibilities, but I want to add another sex drive contributor here. Guess what that might be.

Chapter 6

Just ZIPPING Around Town

I have certainly run into some people who aren't very concerned about their partner's economic contribution (**ZIPPY**), but I haven't reached a conceptual understanding of why. I'm a huge fan of one partner child-rearing while the other partner earns the primary income. That feels equal. I'm also a huge fan of both partners helping with income contribution and child-rearing. That can also result in a nice volley back and forth. But the dynamic that is really hard to conceptualize is where one person is running themselves into the ground, literally carrying all the economic survival weight, while the other partner contributes nothing at all. I guess I have heard of these types of noncontributors as "house" people. They aren't rearing children because the children attend school for most of the day or their children are grown and gone. They are dinking around the house, which involves feeding the dog, or maybe cleaning sometimes, or maybe they are there to accept packages, but these items don't really seem to "earn" their keep. Different strokes for different folks though.

I'm not talking about people who stay at home, unable to contribute because they are disabled. Being genuinely disabled—because a doctor has signed off on a physical, mental, cognitive, behavioral, or other disability—is a real reason for a lacking contribution. Actually not being able to contribute is very different than *choosing* not to. Similar to saying no to sex, we can't just choose not to contribute in order for a partnership to work.

Let me share why I am so worried about "house" people. Having a partner who actually can carry all the weight is amazing. Props to the house people for finding someone who is absolutely killing it. But I feel like there's an inherent vulnerability with people who are capable of doing everything on their own. They have a hard time finding partners. Why? Because it is really easy to intimidate other people when you're fully capable of caring for yourself. People wonder what they have to offer you if you are fully taking care of yourself. So these types of people are susceptible to other people who can't care for themselves or have chosen not to. People who are successful want someone to care for and people who can't care for themselves want someone to care for them. I get it. I can 100 percent care for myself. I know that, and there's a confidence attached to that which has, in the past, impaired my ability to get a quality partner. I did attract abusive men or men who needed to be rescued. Neither of which will make good partners.

People are typically attracted to very different people, but people typically don't want someone who is functioning at a significantly higher level. The gap can't be so large that one person always feels like the weakest link. I'm not saying that successful people are intentionally trying to be better or advertising themselves as better. Typically, people who have done some work on themselves want other people who push them to be better, but they don't typically want to surround themselves with people who chronically make them feel less than. I often hear that house people don't feel threatened by not contributing. Maybe there's either codependence that drowns the typical threatening feeling or having someone take care of them feels normalized. Being fully taken care of as a child almost to the point of being babied will lead to having the same expectations as an adult.

There's probably a chance that house people are defining their identity through their successful partners. So every time their partner achieves a certain milestone, they do too. It becomes a "we" success rather than an individual win. My main concern with this would be that if anything should happen to a house person's partner, they would be utterly destroyed. Their identity is wrapped up in someone else, so not only would they lose their partner, they would also lose their own identity. That can be incredibly scary. Interdependence is always going to be a better answer than codependence.

There's a chance that house people are contributing to the world in a positive way outside of the home, but the contribution at home gets neglected. This is probably a better variation because at least there is passion and a certain degree of independence driving the societal contribution. I worry less about self-destruction if something were to happen to the partner who is fully supporting them. But there's still a big question mark as to why either partner finds this dynamic fulfilling; passion, in any capacity, is a large component in terms of how happy people are. Passion outside of the home could check the box in the same way that passion inside of the home does, but the successful partner will feel the impact of that.

I have also seen the workaholics and how that impacts their ability to show up in the home. The people with more masculine energy are notorious for obsessing about their work. Not only are they typically the primary breadwinner, but they are emotionally enmeshed in the positive reinforcement that work offers, especially if the positive reinforcement at home is minimal at best. I often have conversations with my masculine energy-driven clients about how we have to be careful of the work metric because it's so solid, it is measurable, and objective. It is absolutely addictive.

We only get the best outcome from categories where we invest our best efforts. More investment in work and less of an investment in the home will turn out all the positive effects in the work realm. Once we start down this path, it is hard to check back in. People respond to us checking out in the home with more checking out. And partners and/or kids can be fickle about whether they let you try again after being checked out for so long. It will be a hard transition to include you when you're ready to be mindful and conscientious again.

I would also imagine there's probably a lot of irritability in this space as well. People who invest a lot in their work, me included, tend to get easily overwhelmed when we transition back into the home. It is hard to split exorbitant amounts of effort in two places every day. But the irritability keeps people away from us. I try to remind myself about that often. Or have my husband remind me about it often. Irritability is another version of anger and people can't get close to it without feeling triggered.

Even people without a traumatic past will get triggered by any variations of anger. They will absorb the angry disposition and make it their own or assume that it is about them. Already feeling angry and dealing with someone's reaction to it on top of that is one of the hardest things on the planet to deal with. So I like to see something that allows for regaining our composure before we transition into the home after work. It isn't our partner's fault that we have chosen to make work such an exceptional priority. And if we do happen to slip up for taking it out on them, apologize and commit to do better. For me, it's meditation and HOP WTR (a non-alchoholic sparkling water with mood-boosting ingredients), but you do you.

I see the same effect happen with people who are unable to maintain steady employment. Excluding people who are genuinely disabled again, these people have incredibly short durations at work. There's typically a series of external blame that sound like I hated my boss, or people were mean to me, or the pay wasn't sufficient, or they didn't pay me on time. Maybe the reasons are the same each time, or maybe they are a little different each time, but the outcome is the same. Being unemployed is way more consistent than being employed. Watch out for these folks because there's a high probability inconsistency will show up in other categories. Their complaints are taking precedence over the ability to work through adversity. When things get tough, this person might bail. This is an incredibly frustrating characteristic that will send people on an unexpected roller coaster.

So no economic contribution isn't the answer. But what does a healthy volley look like?

I have a couple who weighed the pros and cons of putting their baby in daycare and realized quickly that the mom could stay at home without much of a financial loss to the family structure. While I can't imagine myself ever being capable of staying at home full-time, I give this couple so much credit. There's some fine tuning that we are doing, but the mom finds so much passion and purpose in raising her kid. The dad finds so much passion and purpose in making money for the household. So when they come together, they get to share all about their passion and purpose in their own designated roles. The dad travels often, so there are plenty of times where the mom is completely solo, but when he comes home he jumps into all the open categories to help. So while both partners are nailing their own roles, they also interchange roles according to what positively enhances the family culture. They are parallel playing at a similar pace while being responsible for completely different things.

From my experience, the most difficult thing about volleying economic contributions back and forth is the transition into and out of our typical contributions. For example, I have a husband who travels fairly frequently. When he is traveling, I'm responsible for so many economic contributions. Not that he isn't making economic contributions while he's traveling, but my contributions increase dramatically in his absence. After a week or two of doing everything, I have developed a flow that works quite nicely for everyone. I'm hustling and working my tail off, but there's a rhythm. When he comes home, he desperately wants a place in the family structure. But there's no room. I have developed a rhythm of doing all the things myself. And remember, I have an avoidant attachment style. I can do *all* the things, hear me roar. So it has worked a little better to have specific things that he can always insert himself into. Trash, laundry, dishwasher, kid drop-off and pickup seem to be the best tickets to success. But the flow works best when we compete for economic contributions (in a playful way), and we have happily jumped into deficiencies with the goal of making them better.

This makes me think about physically distanced couples because of work, the military, lack of financial resources, controlling family, religious values, etc. Physical distance puts a wrench in the side of a partnership that is trying to aim for an equitable economic distribution. We are a military family and I feel like I can attest to this experience pretty well. But I'm pretty big about keeping my husband in the know. The more details, the better here, so it is almost like he's involved with the everyday grind in the same way that I am.

For example, my son woke me up at 2 a.m. to tell me that he puked everywhere. Great. I'm the world's worst human to wake up at night. Mainly because I'm an eight-hour lady in order to be the best version of myself. So…I went to check out the damage and discovered a massacre in the bathroom. The red peppers, bright red tomatoes, and long penne noodles from last night's dinner had been chucked everywhere. Everything in our bathroom is white. The tile, shower curtain, toilet, bath, sinks—everything is white. I texted my husband and he called it, "real exorcism stuff." Obviously he can't clean up with me, but moral support was there 100 percent. Distance coupling isn't an opportunity to check out. It's an opportunity to check in harder.

In my husband's line of work and in many of our friends' lines of work, there are volunteer opportunities. When I say volunteer, I mean it is not required but absolutely looks good for your next career move. So there's probably an unsaid demand or unsaid requirement here, but the amount of people who had partnerships on the rocks and would also volunteer was always concerning. We all know that military relationship stats aren't good, closely related to the poor stats with the police, firefighters, and pilots, so why intentionally add more pressure? Once again, I think it goes back to what do you want more, career notoriety or a happy, healthy partnership? You can have both, but if I shared what that requires, it would be pretty unappealing for most people. Plus, I go back to the meme about how nobody is going to remember how good you were at your job, but everyone will remember how you made them feel. Volunteer for more time away sometimes, but also counterbalance that with a trip with your partner so you can reconnect, just you and them.

Or pay for someone to help your partner when you're away. I have this amazing client who sees me because he wants to show up in a better way for his wife. He doesn't want to leave any rock unturned in how other men might be showing up for their partners. So we talked about how his wife's maternity leave will end after twelve weeks and she's hesitant about returning to work. So how did we decide to make that transition easier for her, since his job is so demanding? He is going to buy flowers on a regular rotation and offer that they get a cleaner every other week instead of once a month. He's thinking ahead and installing more moments of caring for her because he can't be there to fulfill that role.

Money isn't a problem for this last couple I referenced. So if money is a problem, we just have to get a little more creative. Asking a relative to make a meal and bring it over, asking a friend to have your kids over for a playdate, sending a handwritten note are all within the spirit of economically contributing in a financially sound way from a distance. As long as doing nothing extra isn't the answer, distance coupling can be a no-brainer.

Did I also mention that I'm a huge fan of delegating? Yep. I'm big on asking for help for the things that aren't of interest to me. "Hey! There's an e-bill, or a tax document, or a notice that feels too technical. What can you do?" I send my husband PDFs all the time of different mail items that I've scanned that I'd prefer to stick in the fireplace than actually deal with. Impressive that I even remember to check the mail, though, because that's his thing. Help me from a distance, please :). Or help me help myself from a distance. Let me tell you about the new handyman that I just hired for odd jobs around the house.

I also knew a couple who chose to live distanced so one could pursue their dreams in New York and the other one could hang back in the more casual Colorado vibes. They had a budget that would intentionally go toward little Uber Eats deliveries. They would get their partner smoothies, coffees, sandwiches, favorite dinners unprompted and unexpected, so there was a constant exchange of economic contribution toward the relationship space. Little inexpensive gestures that went a long way.

So I promised that all of this was incredibly connected to the frequency and/or intensity of sex. I don't know about you, but there's nothing more sexy than a partner who finds a great deal of pride, self-esteem, or self-worth in their contribution. I also find it incredibly sexy for a partner to have no limits in terms of what they are willing to contribute. You want me to contribute by picking up dog shit? I mean that sucks, but if it is for the greater good, sure. Or you would like to have some time for yourself and the kids are working on the fifth emotionally dysregulated sesh of the day? Give me a lifeline, but I'll figure it out. The fridge is empty, there's no Instacart on its way, and the whole house is screaming at me to concoct something spectacular? Other dads can do this, so why can't I? I love that meme that says "I don't understand the husbands that say no. I could literally bring home a family of whale sharks and my husband would say this is inconvenient, but I'll start building the aquarium." I think that self-sufficiency is an incredibly amazing economic contribution.

I also find it incredibly sexy to have two people to bounce economic contribution problems off of. For example, I have quite a few couples where one of the partners is earning the main living, but their partner is earning a side living. So while reflecting on these couples with this dynamic where the main living partner lost their job, the partner with the side living was able to up the ante quite a bit. Because it has always been a volley of economic contribution, one partner can fill in the deficiencies for the other (at least for a temporary period of time). Maybe there's even a certain amount of pride associated with stepping into making the main income realm if that's not typically the case. Both parties are responsible for the economic contribution and both parties are responsible for fixing the deficiency, already having been practicing the skill of jumping in.

Another thing with economic contribution and finances that is bound to spice up the bedroom will always be the future forward-thinking and planning. So it is great to have regular powwows about where we are right now, but both parties being involved in where we are headed happens to be top-notch. I know so many couples where one partner handles the finances and the other partner has no clue what is going on. This isn't good. Some divorces either happened or were about to happen because one of the partners had no clue what was going on financially or got locked out altogether. It will be incredibly challenging to stand on your own feet when you don't have a clue as to what is available to you because you haven't been paying attention.

It also makes for substantially better conversations about budgeting and/or restrictions if we know the incoming and outgoing flow of money. I think most couples will hit a financial snag at some point in their relationship and to avoid becoming a divorce statistic, it is good to have the mindset that we are both typically responsible for getting ourselves into financial ruin and we are both responsible for getting ourselves out. Remember when I said that very different people find each other most of the time? Well, couples tend to be incredibly different in terms of how they approach money. So because of this large difference, it is entirely practical that there's going to be a higher amount of tension in this space.

My dad spent money like it was going out of style. If I were to guess, I would argue that he never had a budget, not a day in his life. He could have certainly benefited from having one, but that was never on the radar for him. He was also the main person overseeing the finances, which was probably what led to financial ruin for our family at different points of our life. I think the restrictive spender, my mom in this case, needed to be part of the equation in a more substantial way. I'm not sure that would have reduced my dad's spending, but I do think it could have increased mindfulness in that space. Just a check and balance system that would have said, "Hey, we have this basket of bills on the horizon, and we also need to have a rainy day fund." Because there are only rainy days when you're least prepared, but it feels like they happen with more frequency and intensity when you're already financially struggling. By the restrictive spender not paying attention to the day-to-day incoming and outgoing flow, they can't act in a preventative maintenance sort of way. There's only room for exploding when we learn that we aren't making ends meet.

In my own relationship I'm the spender, but I'm also not solely responsible for managing our finances. In fact, I probably only do 25 percent, if I were to be completely honest. Mainly because I am running a business and I am solely responsible for managing money on that side of the fence. I don't have the time to jump over into the personal realm all that often, but you better believe I know the basics and I can access every single account that we own. I have the account numbers, routing numbers, passwords, know approximately how much money is in them and when I should get worried about their status. I know all of my husband's personal information including social security, obviously birth date, log ins, app access, computer access, phone access, how to send a code to one of the spots and be able to access it so I can conduct my searches accordingly. I want to know enough to be able to support myself if we had to throw in the towel, but I don't want to know so much that I impede on his strength. My husband loves numbers, spreadsheets, equations, budgeting, and planning for the future. He finds pride in that space. He literally went to school for these things. I went to school for psychology, where mathematics was supposed to be left out. I was the idiot who decided to get my doctorate, though, and stats got brought right back into my dissertation. So disappointing.

So I have to admit that I hate budgeting. Not just because I am a spender and spenders want to be free to spend accordingly. But also because every time I hear about one person budgeting in the couple structure, the other partner is throwing a huge fit. I don't know if it is because the budgeter also likes to control other categories in addition to finances or if the budgeter is presenting the budget in the worst way possible, so as not to sell their partner on the operation. We spend more time trying to fix the fit that the non-budgeter is throwing than we spend coming up with a plan to save money. So typically the budget doesn't even make it through the starting gates.

So you're probably wondering what the best tactic is. I'm wondering the same thing myself, but I have discovered that budgets work best when couples pair them with lifestyle changes that align with the budget restrictions. So for example, skiing is an incredibly expensive activity. It can be fun, exhilarating, and right in alignment with living a full life.

But for couples on a budget, it probably doesn't make sense. So instead of saying something like, "You can't go skiing because it is not in our budget", I would say something like, "It probably makes the most sense that we eliminate all the heavy hitters: skiing, boating, traveling, partying, and going out to eat." We need to get our partner's buy-in as to what we are going to eliminate from our lifestyles either temporarily or more permanently before the request to do those things comes in to hit us in the face.

It is not a criticism to discuss a preventative measure plan about everything that is being eliminated before the temptation sets in. Waiting until after the temptation sets in to say no and then belittling our partners for not staying in the budget is absolutely a criticism and will be treated as such. Moving a spender away from spending is an art and needs to be treated delicately. Asking them to do a very specific thing during a powwow gives some degree of delegation, and it gives them a chance to want to feel responsible for the financial trajectory that the couple structure has chosen.

I like to encourage couples to tell their partner what they want more of. It is a positive request rather than a negative statement. Something like, "Would you mind going to the regular grocery store rather than Whole Foods because of the price difference?" Literally a question I get all the time. If it is presented in a way that says, "Changing this one particular habit could contribute positively to the budget rather than you always making moves that put us further into debt", I'm totally gonna buy in.

This gets tricky though. Because not only do spenders and savers find each other. But also people who want to live a lifestyle of the rich and famous find humble and kind folks to settle down with. I'm a spender and that directly syncs up with a showy lifestyle. My husband is a saver and may or may not wear clothes he wore in high school as a soon-to-be forty-year-old man. So how in the world are we supposed to get these jokers to sync up? Well, with an incredibly delicate path. I've found that it works best to have a global plan. My husband knows that I want a Mercedes GLE Coupe when I currently drive a Volvo XC90. Both are nice cars, but there's probably a $50,000 difference in price, and I'm not quite sure that our 100 lb. dog can fit in the back of the GLE. So instead of saying that I'm ridiculous and the GLE is never going to be in the cards for us, he says, "You double your income this year, and I fully support that purchase."

I think we run into problems with hard nos in most categories. But lifestyle preferences and what someone is accustomed to is certainly a category that doesn't do well with no. My husband used to say no quite often. But then I would badger him relentlessly until he submitted. That's a lot of work for me and probably was a nightmare for him. So instead, he's replaced the verbiage with something more positive: when this lines up, so will that extravagant purchase. He will throw no fits when the time comes that I've doubled my income and the GLE is in the cards. Maybe this seems a little unfair, but I do believe that the spender and/or the partner with the extravagant lifestyle needs to be incentivized for the behavior to improve. Honestly, the incentive I receive is a motivator to push harder. Right? If I push harder in my career (which actually benefits me), the couple structure is there to reward the system. That feels like an all-around win for everyone. My husband actually benefits by doubling my income too. Not that he will buy anything, of course, but he will be super stoked to see the dollar numbers rise in our account.

I want to avoid the economic contribution and finances becoming too much of a tit for tat. I think it is easy to be in a relationship and want to win. It is easy to be competitive with your partner. A healthy level of this seems okay. There are times, in jest, either one of us will brag about making the most money for the year. It is relatively hard to say who will come in first place because both of us have multiple gigs going on at the same time. But that little piece of competition feels good. I have heard other couples taking it a bit too far with either demeaning the lower-producing partner or demanding that the spending habits of both partners is in direct alignment with how much they pull in. Meaning that your allowance is dictated by the amount coming in. Or percentages are driven by your contribution to the pot. You can do this, but my guidance is this: we can quickly put someone in safety mode, especially someone who has experienced trauma, by equating their worth to a tangible economic contribution. Once we put someone in safety mode, it is more challenging to get them out than never to allow them to get there in the first place.

I also want to comment about how some people will tell themselves that they are fine with the state of the economic contributions, and during a moment when they let down their guard (caused by substances, trauma, grief/loss), they will blast their partner with how they actually feel about it. Best to reach a place that you can hang your hat on. Do you want to be happy or do you want to win? There are going to be parts of relationships where we just have to leave it alone, we just have to agree to disagree, and move on because there are bigger fish to fry that need our time and attention. To me, economic contributions and financial resources should be regularly attended to when they are little fish, so they don't eventually turn into bigger fish.

People who have been reared in a home that wasn't mindful of economic contribution and financial resources typically turn out with one of two ways of coping. They either remain in the childhood survival mode that they were taught, or they completely reject that norm and start winging it, spending outside of their means. People who are mimicking their childhood because they don't know any other way and the scarcity model seems like a good landing space, are incredibly hard-headed. Anytime someone has spent a long time mimicking their childhood history and they have been in survival mode for so long, we should expect that their rigidity is born out of survival and is probably here to stay. Talking someone out of survival mode into higher levels of functioning, belonging, happiness, and self-actualization feels impossible. Sometimes it feels easier to rein in someone who is winging it (doing the opposite of their childhood) because they have broken free from the confines of their earlier trauma to find a new way. And they probably want to learn all about the best way.

We can't force our partners to change if they aren't ready, but we can find some grace for their rigidity if we understand where it came from and our partners acknowledge that the roots are a little deeper than average. My guiding light is that some rigidity in some categories can probably be worked through or worked around, but rigidity in most categories is a very different story. We need to be able to present to our partners the way that we think is best. Our partner needs to present the finances in the way they think is best. And then we start the negotiations, so we can land in a space where nobody feels on top of the world, but nobody feels screwed over either.

Sometimes the partner who is struggling with rigidity came from a childhood home that is still actively involved in their life. Meaning they have a parent and/or caregiver who is still so actively involved that the partner can't grow and change according to their own individual desires or the desires of the couple structure. People can be so attached to their childhood and all the key players that it leaves no room for a partner to get in there.

Receiving money from our parents as an adult toys with our conceptualization of who we are. Are we putting on a show to earn our caregiver's economic contribution or are we receiving money that's independent from our performance. A lot of people who have real, regular money coming in from caregivers and don't have to economically contribute on their own could also have to behave in a particular way that doesn't work for the partnership. Keep an eye out for this because it often results in the partner and the parent competing for the time, attention, and affection of the trapped grown adult. While the trapped grown adult might not worry about the competition, it is rather awful competing for this as the partner.

Another area I want to touch on briefly are the people who have worked their tails off to retire early. I'm not talking about those who retire in their fifties or sixties. I'm talking about retiring in their thirties and forties. Amazing that someone has hustled so hard to get to that point, and I'm certainly jealous, but how is the time spent? I think there's a lot of extra space when someone isn't working in any capacity, and I'm very interested in exactly how that extra space is filled up.

There are a couple options here, which essentially tie into my next point. The first option is that the space is filled up with self-interest activities. While self-interest activities aren't the end of the world and actually quite beneficial in a lot of ways, self-interest activities can keep us away from interdependence. Self-interest activities include solo sports (skiing, hiking alone, running competitions, going to the gym), drinking and/or using drugs alone, obsessing over eating clean or the cleanliness of our surroundings. Like I said, some of these solo activities are quite healthy in moderate levels. But any of these items left unchecked by a partner, by someone else, or by a group of people leads to a lack of mindfulness about the community.

Also, too many self-interest activities for a long period of time typically create too much rigidity in someone's ability to make room for a partner. Bachelors and bachelorette folks are great, but only for a designated period of time. I've certainly seen the younger age groups in their twenties or thirties land on someone forty-plus, or a first relationship failing in someone's late thirties only to find someone forty-plus who hasn't practiced the art of making space for someone else. I really do consider it an art because my personality left unchecked or without challenge would happily settle into an unchanging groove that is pretty much solidified now that I'm almost forty. If you're also in that age range or older, I would bet some money that you've established a pretty cool routine that works for you and you have very little interest in completely overhauling something that works for you. I totally get it. But having a healthy partnership requires that you rearrange, so once again, I'm interested in someone's mental flexibility as you start to merge lives.

For those of you who are into the popular reality TV series *Married at First Sight,* Virginia and Erik are trying to merge their lives, and it's rough! Virginia loves her cats like other people love their kids. The cats sleep in the bed and have free-rein of Virginia's home. Erik is incredibly allergic to cats and has a pretty hard line in the sand about the cats not being in his bedroom space. Also, Virginia is very interested in being social and partying with or without Erik. Erik has left that lifestyle behind him and just wants to settle down. There's so much back and forth about these issues because two people have already solidified their routine, and they are significantly less flexible than other people who haven't nailed down their routine. In the end, the cats end up in a guest room when

Virginia moves into Erik's place. I'm not sure that the partying decreased at all. Virginia was pretty firm on keeping that intact. But I also just looked up their circumstances and they are divorced. So how much of their rigidity led to the divorce, or were they never meant to be at all? Who knows, it's reality TV after all.

But retiring early can also make people the biggest rockstars of partners. The rigidity hasn't kicked in yet, there's plenty of space to make room for a partner, and they are constantly investing in the community around them. Mad props to these folks because, to me, that is the ultimate experience of self-actualization. Living a life where your work doesn't completely define your identity. Or doesn't define your identity at all. In fact, the absence of work frees up space to love hard, give often, and get to a space where your main mission is to pay it forward. I don't come across these types very often, but when I do, I am a sponge, absorbing all of their material and finding ways to make it my own. If I weren't working, I would have so much space, and I am incredibly interested in what I would end up doing with it.

Ultimately the answer isn't that you can contribute nothing. One partner can't handle all the weight, or if they have thus far, it will eventually come to a close. That will be a really bad day for everyone. But it's important that we don't invest more in the economic contribution space than we do in our partnerships. Remember, whatever we invest in is the thing that comes to fruition. We need to salvage that energy for the transition into the romantic space. Be malleable and change with your surroundings. Have a desire to meet your partner in the gray zone.

So the golden question here is whether we can instill economic contribution after we realize it's not equal. It depends on the partner's willingness to recognize that the weight is unequal. It also depends on the level of empathy they have for the one who carries all the weight. Here are some general ideas:

- Start small, but work toward a bigger goal. (Eventually we want you to get a job, but today and for several days we are working on a resume.)
- Stay away from shame. That's a nasty little bugger. Instead, ask for what you want. Do you want them to earn money or is there a household bigger picture thing that you want them to do?
- Bring in feelings of sadness or fear. (Stay away from anger or variations of anger.) "I feel incredibly lonely raising kids by myself all day."
- Think about solutions before you present the problem. "Hey, we are running low on cash, but I

thought that either I could get a second job, you could pick up more shifts, or we could think about finding more childcare so we could do both."

- ➢ Give positive reinforcement when you do see efforts being made toward economic contribution, otherwise the partner will lose incentive for its value.

Part of economic contribution can be the role that we maintain in the community. As long as it's a contribution that benefits people outside of ourselves.

But we are looking to have an overflow after we meet our own needs, so that we can contribute positively to our relationship space.

Chapter 7

What it Means to be LIKEABLE

This brings me to a conversation about giving back to the community by paying it forward. Being **LIKABLE**. I think I would be a little worried if someone didn't have any work space filling up their time and they weren't giving back to the community in some way. This could be something little like volunteering at a food bank for the holidays or something more major like teaching a certain skill to young people, volunteering at an animal shelter, or offering to help people get a job in their own career field. My husband's aunt is retired and assists in the training of dogs for people with disabilities. I can't imagine a more rewarding and fulfilling way to give back to this world. I think you could hang your hat on that.

But people with an abundance mentality—that there's enough to go around for everyone if you really want it—are better partners than the ones who believe that scarcity is a better way to go. Whereas abundance brings freedom, creativity, and unlimited growth, scarcity makes people scared, biased, and discriminatory.

So we have to think about how someone who believes in abundance would behave. I would imagine that they have a regular practice of gratitude to make sure they don't overlook the little things they already have. I would imagine that their partners pop up on their gratitude lists on a regular basis and they probably convey that gratitude in a way that their partners could conceptualize. They might be mindful of economic contribution, but they certainly aren't greedy or stingy. The willingness to give to their partners on the regular is also probably on their minds. I also imagine that people who think with abundance know that whatever they give is bound to come back to them in leaps and bounds. Taking life a little less seriously and having more of a sense of humor makes taking the lemons that life gives us and turning them into lemonade a little easier.

Optimists feel like there's power behind looking through a positive lens and tend to show more grace when people, especially their partners, disappoint them. Living a life of abundance is a choice, but it is a hard one.

The easier road is scarcity. Sometimes this is a trauma response. Sometimes people watch a lot of other people around them practice scarcity. In my profession, I see this one all the time. I think it comes so naturally because if you pay attention to the negative energy in this world, it seems to multiply. Before we know it, we become sucked down a vortex. People are critical of others because they have been told they weren't good enough. They have gone down the road and gotten shut down. They have lost a loved one. Friends have left them or continue to leave them. Romantic partnerships are harder to find and if they do find them, they aren't hanging around. It makes sense that they feel lousy after the deck was stacked against them, but they just continue to get bogged down by the undertow. The amount of weight that this way of viewing economic contribution puts on partnerships is pretty astronomical and something to pay attention to. This mindset tends to show up in multiple categories of people's lives.

What do you think is the greatest downside to the scarcity mindset? Thinking about its pervasive nature and all.

A scarcity mindset, negativity, and pessimism—these bad boys are all buzz killers, and any relatively healthy person who has worked on themselves won't touch them with a ten-foot pole. Sad, I know. And the person with these mindsets has no idea why it is so hard to land on people in the right way or invest in the relationship in a way that the other person is happy about or is able to to keep deeper-level intimate partnerships. I would imagine that nobody is brave enough to let these types of people into their constructive feedback circle. People are scared of rejection and they are also scared of being the rejector and what blowback will ensure from making the first move.

I don't really imagine anything harder than running into someone who 1) has no clue what about them is driving people away and 2) probably is not going to be open to constructive feedback that they might be hearing for the first time. So I do think about what you have probably thought about before. Since this person could clearly benefit from the feedback, could I be the one to change them? Will I be the one who cracks the secret code? My answer is maybe. This could go one of two ways. The first way is that your feedback strikes a cord with them, they get defensive, emotionally dysregulated, maybe they stop talking to you for a while or even cut you off temporarily. But they spend some time considering the accuracy of your feedback. Maybe they even consider some evidence that supports or refutes it. They eventually come back to you with their conceptualization of the feedback because they know you love and care for them. The second option is that they blame you for being so fucking inconsiderate and rant about how everyone else loves them and you're the only one who seems to be missing that memo. Of course, the best case is blowback with reflection. Worst case is that they can't wait to get the only person who feels adversely about them out of their life so they can go back to believing everyone loves them.

If you look at someone's family of origin, you typically see where the buzz killers started. Even though this is frowned upon and my husband made it very clear on our first date that I wasn't allowed to analyze his mom, I am very interested in who ran the household. Like I have shared before, I love it when both partners pick up the slack where they see fit. Or multiple caregivers are jumping in to fulfill a multitude of different needs. But there's typically a dominant figure in the home that provides the rough outline of how the family organization is going to operate. That key figure has the ability to set the tone of the house. To go back to my black and white themes because I think they are easier to conceptualize, the dominant figure is big on stability or big on emotional dysregulation. Harder for me to see that there's a gray area where both of those two concepts line up together.

When I think about a stable tone, I think about having positive outlets where we can redirect negative energy before it clusters and seeps through the veins of household organizational structure. Is it always showing up as stable and put together? Definitely not. But I do think it's a tone that family members can rely on. The train derails on occasion, but nobody in the home needs to activate something inside themselves for the train to get back on the tracks organically. There's no real panic in terms of when/if the train gets back on the tracks. I've learned that this stability can be fake and it can be real and the end game is still the same. People thrive in environments that offer stability. When I talk about fake stability, I am talking about redirecting negative energy in a "stuffing it" sort of way. I'm talking about using substances or alcohol as a means of stuffing the feelings that might be big and bold enough to rock stability to its core. It is using substances enough to dull the emotional content, but not so much that you can't achieve the functional image you are striving for. It is a tricky balance, but it is referred to as functional alcoholism or a functional drug user. All your daily tasks stay the same with a certain pattern of substance use.

Does it have to be substances that numb the emotional content? Nope. It is the most popular one, but certainly not the only one. There's behind the scenes gambling, porn, cheating, video games, social media obsession. All kinds of things. But people rally behind stability because it feels controllable. Even if you achieve it because of something dysfunctional, controllable is the antithesis to chaotic, so people feel like they are winning. Stability, even if it is fake, gains a lot of notoriety. People on the outside respect stable people way more than they will ever respect chaos. Stable brings bills that get paid, people who show up, and completions of projects. It is consistency and loyalty that create a system of reliability.

Research supports that fake stability is just as meaningful as real stability. It's one of the few psychological concepts that carries more weight in the end game than it does in the journey along the way. But real stability says that even if the train derails, this dominant figure is talking about the recognition of the train derailment, why they think it derailed, and how they plan to solve it in the future. So providing the rationalization for the stability feels like it has a higher capacity for people to absorb it as a legitimate way of functioning. People are concerned about the outcome again here. When we find a partner who comes from this stable dominant figure, you see them show up in their authentic form, you see higher levels of self-esteem, you see a drive toward passion, you see a full community, and you also see mental flexibility. Why? Because we don't achieve anything better than safety and security if we don't have safety and security. Safety and security are the money makers.

My in-laws are probably the most stable set of people that I have ever met in my life. They make my family look like complete and total mayhem. I don't know how long they have been married exactly, but I want to say it is forty-five-plus years. And their routine as a couple and as a family is arguably the exact same from when my husband was reared.

My father-in-law is incredibly passionate about his work as a custom home builder. He's like a fine wine, only getting better and more refined in his knowledge and expertise through the years. He didn't have much to do with the daily grind of raising kids, claiming he can count the amount of times he changed diapers on one hand. But my husband remembers all the things that his dad made sure he experienced. All the sports, activities, and experiences that his dad advocated for. He was present, conscientious, and had an air of competition that actually made my husband good at many things.

My mother-in-law ran the home. She worked for part of my husband's childhood, but she was mainly home connecting all the dots. When dinner was happening, what the sides would be, who had what activity and where it was supposed to be. She made sure her kids were challenged, but she also defended them when the world tried to crush them. My mother-in-law is in the know. She pays attention to what everyone needs, how they operate, and how best she can place herself for a smooth-running machine. Accountability? One hundred percent. My husband describes a disappointed dad look from his dad and a similar response from his mom. Bad behavior had appropriate consequences that nobody argued with. My in-laws positively reinforced good behavior, but bad behavior was met with a "We are your parents. Not your friends." Firm, fair, and consistent in the same way that research supports.

If I ever got into a bind and it didn't have anything to do with harming their golden son, they would be first on my list to call. They are a constant in a really chaotic world.

But what does the flip side look like?

Unless we refuse to accept the same chaos that we grew up with into our world, it will most likely infiltrate into how we perceive the world. I guess that is what is so cool about having the freedom to choose what we will accept into our world and what we will push to keep as part of the childhood chapter only. While people who have been reared in chaos deserve a little bit of grace for the extra hurdle they have up ahead, I don't think it is great to use that excuse in our adult partnerships. In fact, one of the coolest experiences is when a partner who was raised in stability syncs up with a partner who was raised in chaos and the partner who was raised in chaos is ready and willing to learn how they can choose to behave. Using the differences as a learning experience rather than a threat.

Chaos makes people feel as though they have no influence on the way in which life presents itself. And the condition of their partnerships is just an extension of that mentality. If we have no control over anything, then why bother? In actuality, it is the mindset that drives the series of unfortunate events. The more we catastrophize over the series of unfortunate events, the more we see those events flow in. So I think it is important to watch for people who have this victim mentality where the world is out to harm them, because you'll see this translate into other areas of showing up for the community. It all starts with thinking the world is out to get them, and then they put restrictive behaviors in place to prevent intersections.

Contrary to popular opinion, we actually need other people. I would even take this further into a world where we only learn about ourselves through other people. We don't learn how to resolve conflict, or how to develop team-oriented solutions, or how to be vulnerable, raw, and transparent by hanging out with ourselves. We learn through others about our attachment styles, the tone with which we use to communicate, how aggressive we are, what we do with our body language. Once we go down the road of all people are out to get us, or even specific genders are somehow worse than others, we have to keep ourselves away from other people who might potentially challenge that belief structure.

I get it though. I was hosting a couple's workshop this evening and during the Q&A, one of the couples was asking what we should do with introverts who land on an extroverted partner. Great question. I think different people find each other most of the time. But there's a difference between organically recharging alone because people can be overstimulating and overwhelming and intentionally avoiding people because nobody wants to buy into your outrageous, largely negative, complaint-oriented wild hairs. People can recharge alone *and* also believe the world is a relatively decent spot to exist. Should introverts get outside of their comfort zones and hang with people sometimes? Yes. But I can't imagine that the introverted type is thinking about how awful the people are.

The other side of this is that not only do we need other people to teach us about ourselves, but we also need to offer something to the world. It can be little or it can be big, but we need to offer the world a little something extra than if we never existed at all. If we believe the world is bad, we aren't going to be super pumped to pay it forward. When we feel intimidated by others, we probably want to make a significantly lower investment than someone who feels fueled by other people.

So what is something little that we could do to give back to the world? I think about throwing a birthday celebration for a loved one, helping someone else feel special because of our efforts. Or going out of our way to be mindful and present with people when we are offering them our quality time. Holding doors for people. Showing people that we are grateful for them and their contribution. Lending a helping hand to someone in need. When I think about the bigger ticket items, I think about pursuing a career that we are passionate about, but also that contributes positively to the well-being of the world. Something that makes a difference. Or passing along a skill, a tool, or a positive attribute that positively benefits the world.

I think people who understand this concept—that the world is bigger than only being concerned about our individualized needs—are better partners. Going outside of ourselves can be demonstrated in a wide array of different ways, so it doesn't seem to be how we go outside of ourselves as much as just having the ability to think about the impact, positive or negative, that we have on the world. People go outside of themselves by finding their identity through their community, by participating in religious organizations, by embarking on spiritual explorations, by praying, or by meditating. All of these sources are connections to something greater than we live and we die, which gives up the mental flexibility to make concessions for others.

We need to have some sort of relationship with something greater than ourselves, and we also need separate friends and relationships outside of our partner. I see this dynamic fairly often. One of the partners prefers to spend every waking moment with their partner while the other one prefers more of a balance, some time together coupled with some time with outside relationships. The more one partner asks for friend or family time, separate from their partner, the more the other partner clings on. Maybe the original partner has fears of abandonment, insecurity, or anxiety could be part of that. Maybe the partner who wants the outside relationships is up to naughty things. But both partners need to have their own set of relationships separate from each other, and we need to have the freedom and space to invest in those dynamics.

We also have to be trustworthy when we spread our wings in the community. I think there are some people who overdo it in the community space, which can pull from the relationship space. It is probably easier for someone who is extroverted to overdo it in the community space and sometimes boundaries can get violated with too many outside influences. Frankly, there's nothing cooler than both partners spreading their wings to a certain degree but also making it incredibly clear that they are taken, have to be home by a certain time, and talk a big game about their partner when they are out and about. Being separate from our partners isn't always easy, especially if we are talking about long-distance relationships, so I always encourage them to think about what their partner would want. Are they behaving in a way that respects their partner?

So community involvement is key. It's bigger than just being a part of a community entity. It is investing something special about yourself back into the world around you. Money shouldn't be an exchange for everything because the world is bigger than us. People who think of others outside of themselves will always be better partners. So it's especially unique when, as we pull back from work, we drive harder into the space where other people benefit from our existence.

If your partner says fuck the community, what can we do? Get a new partner. Kidding. Kind of. But a willingness to change this mentality can go a long way. We can offer some suggestions:

- "Hey I know you love animals so much. There's a position at the local animal shelter that opened up and I thought we could both apply if you're open to it."

- "Come give meals to the homeless with me this weekend."

- If your partner has a specialized skill, we could try to pair them with an interested teen in the neighborhood. I see that on Nextdoor all the time.

- Ask your partner if they would be interested in hosting a neighborhood barbecue.

- Talk highly of people you meet in the world. It will certainly rub off on your partner. If you need to reroute negativity, make sure to do so.

So what's the difference between someone who goes out into the world, always to return, and someone who goes out into the world with questionable behaviors and a questionable return status?

Chapter 8

EMPOWERED People Change the World

To me, it is the sense of self. Being **EMPOWERED** by our ability to choose.

Did we come out of our child home all messed up? Was it sprinkled in small moments of trauma? Or was it relatively decent? Because if we keep it relatively simple with these options, the outcomes can be dramatically different. When people are looking for their forever partner(s), they want to know what to look for. Well this is my absolute top pick. Look for someone who understands where they came from and what type of hustle they need to have in order to get to the best version of themselves. And I don't want the messed up childhood folks to think that they got unlucky because nobody walks away from their lives without a hurdle that they spend their life trying to overcome. Those are just the facts. Maybe you had a relatively decent childhood, but you can't find a partner to save your life. Maybe your childhood was only sprinkled in trauma, but you can't figure out what you want to be when you grow up. Hopefully, you're catching on to the fact that we all have stuff going on that we are trying to work out.

So this goes out to the messed up childhood folks. What happened to you wasn't your fault. There are so many reasons why your childhood could have been messed up. A caregiver was a drug addict, an alcoholic, a womanizer, or they didn't protect you from bad people, or they couldn't make ends meet, they got caught up in love with the wrong people, or maybe they died young. Whatever the reason was, the sooner we detach that we were the reason why any of these terrible things happened, the sooner we get to create the newest versions of ourselves.

I love it when someone can plop down in front of another and say, "You know what? My childhood was shitty because I had a mom who was never around. But I understand that she abandoned me because of her own stuff and not because of me. And I also understand that it made me feel sad and lonely and I'm committed to helping my kids not have to feel the sadness that I went through. Just know that abandonment is an issue for me, but I am working my ass off to neutralize the impact." To me, it will always be less about the depths of how bad the thing was that we endured and more about the awesome life lesson that it taught us. And yes, I do believe there's a life lesson in all experiences.

I've seen people come out of messed up childhoods with an ego. We have to keep an eye out for that. Mainly because the ego isn't real in this case. It was created as a defense mechanism to protect people from experiencing repeat pain in the same way that they did in their childhoods. And! We don't always know what is lurking underneath an exacerbated, manufactured ego. It can be debilitating sadness, rage, constant, incessant ruminations. But because the ego is protecting them in overtime mode and preventing them from getting hurt, the side effect can often be that they hurt others. I don't necessarily think this is intentional and there's certainly empathy that goes out to people with this history, but if we drive people away before they have a chance to abandon us, we do get to feel in control. The driving people away thing can be confusing for the person on the receiving end.

We can also walk away from messed up childhoods as a doormat. Because the home was so chaotic and the only thing that was learned was how to keep the peace, people often stopped advocating for their own needs. Well, put that into our adult lives or put that into a partnership and we let other people dictate the path for us. Great that we don't need to carve out our own path or make decisions that we aren't responsible for. But not so great in terms of the probability that one day you will probably wake up and say, "Wow, my life sucks. Let's scratch this version and start over." Having your partner wake up one day to this realization will be the worst day of your life.

There's a chance that we find a sweet spot, between ego and doormat, coming out of childhoods that are messed up, but the stats are incredibly low. These folks are only nailing this objective, most likely, because they have worked their tail off to get there. They have been able to develop an understanding that not everyone is representative of the untrustworthiness of their caregivers. They haven't taken familial experiences as a child and clumped them together to represent a negative global analysis of humankind. They remain malleable in terms of their childhood history being wrong, but they also get that there's so much more to learn. They probably have been able to witness some healthy role models, professionals, peers, other families that have discovered a better way. I love it when people can talk about their findings in a casual way: "Hey, I was dealt a bad deck, but then I found this other group of people that was living in the way that I dreamt about, so I immersed myself in their lives instead."

What about the folks who were sprinkled in some trauma, but came out otherwise unscathed? I think these people can also be a mixed bag. What doesn't traumatize someone at all can severely traumatize someone else with the same experience. We all experience trauma in some form, but the levels of intensity are completely dependent on the individual human. What we see here is the tendency to be inconsistent. Because their childhoods were relatively consistent but also had some mixing and mingling of trauma, the "winging it" mentality can show up as an adult. Having a "let's just wing it and see how it goes, partner" is hard. While you might get some more mindfulness, empathy, kindness, and care, you might not get any values that are wrapped around structure and routine. I don't know about you, but while I would love to wing everything, I don't know how you run a household in this space. It takes every little piece of structure that I can muster in order to ensure that everything gets done. If the school has a delayed start that I've forgotten about, I also forget to feed the dog, or eat breakfast, or do something physical, clients get rescheduled, and if I had any sense of composure before, it is long gone.

We can also see some pretty high achievers come out of this space. Sometimes the opposite of *dabbling in chaos* is perfectionism. While I do think there's a large portion of the population that has these tendencies, a childhood history of intermittent moments of trauma certainly puts these tendencies on overdrive. You'll see people who are workaholics because they get the most positive reinforcement for their perfectionism in the work space. Or we see a certain degree of paralysis that happens if they don't get a chance to checklist all the different items in their routine. Granted, routines make us better, because they are typically representative of what we've learned about our own needs, but being unable to shut down our brains ever will lead to burnout as we head for unrealistic goals.

The amount of growth that we have pursued post-childhood experiences determines who we are and whether we are proud to be in our own shoes. I think it is confusing because people can "peacock" in the beginning of a relationship, sometimes for so long that people actually consider the fact that the person has actually integrated between who they actually are versus who they have the potential to be. But coming out of our childhood home with an emphasis placed on image, it is easy to get transparency and image all mixed up. It is presentation and image that will equate to our success. Doing all the socially acceptable things because that's what successful people do rather than embarking on the value of authenticity. People naturally cater toward areas that they get the most positive reinforcement for and if the image was positively reinforced at home, they have a high likelihood of doing the same.

As a partner it just feels burdensome to constantly be the one that is reining in the other one. Should there be a little bit of difference in styles between the two partners? Absolutely. Should the difference be so great that one of the partners feels like they need to turn into a parent? I think that's where things get tricky to navigate. My husband and I will always be known for how different we are. He's logical and I'm completely irrational. He's thrifty and I'm a spender. He recharges with screen time and I recharge 100 percent alone or entertaining a group of people. I like it hot and he would prefer cold. He sprints and I jog. But we love the hell out of each other and we are completely on board with doing whatever the other wants as long as we get to hang out together. Without the kids is a huge perk.

I think we watch the sense of self come through our primary caregivers and end up picking the set of characteristics in our partners that most closely replicates that dynamic. So if we watched one caregiver give all the orders and the other partner just took the orders, and we are also given more of a docile set of characteristics, we have a tendency to choose someone who gives orders. If we watched someone give orders and we watched someone just take the orders, and we were given a more aggressive personality, we would probably pick someone that isn't interested in confrontation. Obviously there's an innate desire to replicate our upbringing because that feels comfortable, but our personality characteristics will have a lot to do with where we end up.

There's also a chance we saw caregivers interact and we thought, "Yah. That. Whatever they have been doing is exactly what I don't want in my own life." I don't think there's anything wrong with deciding that we want nothing to do with replication. It is just a significantly harder path. And it is a path that we can't take without help. But at the same time, sometimes it feels like the only help around is our partner. I think we look toward our partners to help us define what we want our lives to look like because the examples we were shown were awful ones. Similar to the parent-child dynamic, this can feel like a burden for the partner who is constantly helping recreate this life for their partner that their partner knows nothing about. It's not all bad, but intimate partnerships are a pretty complicated space to learn from. I don't know about you, but there's pretty much nothing that I would enjoy my husband teaching me. And I'm fairly confident he would feel the same way. Sometimes teaching creates too much of a hierarchy where the teacher is put on a higher level than the recipient.

It is a pretty cool thing when we can pull from different areas of our childhood upbringing, decide that we want to keep a few things, and also decide that we will be leaving quite a bit behind. Like I said, less about what we went through and more about how we choose to show up in front of the partnerships we create. I think there are very few humans on the planet who would laugh in our faces if we shared that our childhood history sucked, but that we are doing the best we can to make it better. Staying somewhere in between egotistical and doormat. We don't want to drive everyone away with our self-centered nature, the inability to see outside of ourselves. Nor do we want to get completely run over all the time. People don't respect people who don't demand respect.

What do we do with someone who has a weird sense of self? I have a couple ideas here:

- Ask them if they have come across a particular person in their life that was killing it, just really nailing life. What qualities did they pull from that person?

- It never hurts to reflect on values together. Values line up pretty closely with the sense of self.

- Encourage them to ask others for feedback about themselves. Scary, but every time I ask people what they think about me, I get new data that I haven't thought of before.

➢ Encourage your partner to journal so they are getting the design of their ideals down on a piece of paper.

➢ If they are introverted, put going out in public on the calendar once per month. If they are extroverted, talk them into playing We Are Not Really Strangers at home, just the two of you, for a whole night.

Challenging our partners without making them feel uncomfortable should be the goal here. Which brings me to how cool the next chapter is.

Chapter 9

How DEEP can you go?

Our partners have to have a relatively decent ability to demonstrate **DEPTH.** Depth is what connects us intimately. It is the webbing between all the other concepts we have talked about throughout this book. We need to go deep in our ability to find ourselves. We need to communicate with love. We need to resolve conflict quickly and effectively by understanding that we are here to align and solve problems together. We need to understand why it's important to participate in our partnership. Being frisky says we have the audacity to be bold in front of our partners. We conceptualize that life is greater than just living and dying. We strive to be better than how we were raised even if we can see the flaws in the system. Sure, living on the surface is fine and dandy, but if social media has taught me anything, it's that people connect through adversity far easier than they connect by talking about the weather, work, or the kids.

People want to know what you've been through to get to this point. It is almost like a badge of honor to be in the club. I'll never forget my few years of experience counseling folks who struggled with drugs and/or alcohol addiction. Not that I was on a stage, but if I was on a stage, they would have certainly thrown stuff at me. I haven't experimented with drugs ever. And alcohol is usually the occasional drink socially. So a fish out of water who is trying to help people overcome that kind of addiction having never been down that road myself. Sure, I can relate to the feeling, and usually that is good enough with counseling, but they were pretty disappointed with the lack of experience. Right? People want to know that we've walked down paths with thorns and it obviously didn't kill us.

But this is tricky because you have to have depth without being a whiny face. Incredibly challenging to tow this line. Why? Because sharing about adversity could potentially have no bounds. This happens to me all the time. I'm hanging out with one of my besties, they mention how annoying one of our neighbors is, and bam! Off to the races. I say, "Yah. They are completely inconsiderate, clearly not part of any sort of community, and the nerve!" Right? So this kind of depth of a share might be perfectly within normal limits, but if we then expand on it with, "You know, I've been thinking about how shitty *all* of my neighbors have been. I can't remember a single neighbor who has been respectful to me and my family." So easy to connect with the person who is frustrated with a neighbor, but very easy to get lost amid an extreme that incorporates *all* the neighbors *ever*. It's that easy to take it too far, and depending on who the person is and how easy they are to talk to, you could catch yourself in a downward spiral pretty quickly.

People like to whine and they also like to complain. These two types of people haven't evolved yet. That's not to say that they won't eventually evolve. But right now, as they talk trash about people, places, things, themselves, their own life, it is hard to see them headed for self-actualization. Which, I believe, is a lifelong goal for a lot of people. Even if you never achieve it, you can certainly spend your life aiming for it.

So what happens when you put someone who hasn't evolved into a relationship? Things get pretty unequal pretty quickly. If you also haven't evolved, then you both learn together. Maybe. Although, misery sure does love company. But if someone who has evolved lands on someone who has not, there's so much extra weight to carry. The partner on the receiving end of someone who hasn't evolved will skip going deep if that means also skipping out on the surface-level toxicity they might be barraged with. We can always try to reroute, change the topic, or set specific boundaries, but we might also have to get creative in what we talk about if we aren't planning on complaining. There are very few topics that would set us up for no complaining. I looked this up at one point, and the result was pretty telling.

So the purpose here in going deep isn't complaining as much as it is developing depth that we know our audience can handle, with topics that are either neutral or relatively positive. Reading the room feels like an incredibly important asset here. The amount of couples I see who aren't listening to their partner, who aren't able to assess how they are feeling, and frankly don't have a great track record of paying attention to anything other than themselves, is actually quite shocking. So I feel like this is a real problem.

I'm not sure what exactly happened in terms of falling madly in love with someone and then reaching a place where you're the equivalent of ships passing in the night. But I do want to say that paying attention to your partner is actually pretty complicated. Sorry to bring in my avoidant attachment style again, but remember how we are always taking of ourselves?

I'm a powerful woman, hear me roar type of thing? Well, that actually makes me quite selfish in some ways. Not because I have bad intentions, but because taking care of myself in an exceptional way means that I put all my eggs into that one basket and don't notice my surroundings in my personal life. My professional life, obviously, is a very different story, but I can miss the signs of my husband missing me.

I think his recent "deployment" has been an eye opener for me. I say deployment lightly because he can occasionally visit us, and he is states away rather than countries. But without his check and balance system of "Hey. How are you? How was your day? How were the kids?" I think I would get completely lost in all the things I'm passionate about after the kids go to bed. I love to read, and watch trash TV. I love crime series (although I get scared of the dark when I watch them too much), and getting caught up on work for my private practice. The two hours that fly by in between kid bedtime and my bedtime never seem to last as long as I'd hope. Great that I'm so passionate, right? Not great that I could forget I'm married unless it smacked me in the face. So I lean in as opposed to doubling down and rejecting the outreaches like I would before. I understand that we are better when I pay better attention. My husband, on the other hand, doesn't miss a beat. He gets Google Home notifications on his phone and when he sees me on the cam, he whistles at me. I crack up every time. I sure hope that he knows how much I love him, because I certainly don't show it with as much diligence as he does.

But if we do our best to pay attention to our partner, we won't miss when they make big changes. Big changes can be for the better, of course, but they can also be for the worse. Better moves seem like a healthier eating pattern, or increased physical exertion, or the development of a connection outside of ourselves. But changes that we don't want to miss could also include a hyperfocus on a new, special friend, extra traveling that doesn't seem to be correlated directly to making money, or binging substances more intensely or with a more regular pattern. If we are able to recognize the things for the better right when the change happens, we can get in there and positively reinforce it. My husband was the first person to say, "Wow. I can't believe how much progress you have made with your book." As soon as I had made an announcement that I completed a certain amount of words, he was all up in that positive reinforcement.

The same is true for changes that feel aversive. We can get in there and ask questions about whether or not we need to improve something about our relationship because we've noticed a substantial amount of emotional energy going toward this new friend. Preventative maintenance is key here. The sooner we can get in there and show interest, the sooner we can potentially break up a nasty trajectory.

I also want to bring in the importance of empathy because I think this is pretty easy to miss too. When our partners come to us with anything less than their best, I think we need to show up to support, validate, and be their number one cheerleader. The speed at which I can recover from a pretty intense blow with my husband's help versus without him is impressive. He has a way of neutralizing everything. Because he's logical and I'm irrational, he's very interested in real, concrete evidence I have to support the aversive feeling that I'm having. When I learn that I don't have enough evidence to support my theory, the feeling subsides as well. Without big feelings, my behavior isn't all that bad to combat either. I would like to say that I offer him the same thing, but my disposition is anger, so the odds are that I just get incredibly pissed off at the thing or the person who treated him poorly. If you want me to match your level of intensity, I'm the best cheerleader in town.

It is also cool to see when couples who were a bit more closed off in the earlier part of their relationship continue to blossom over time as they get validated for everything, independent from whether their partner is actually on board with them. Vulnerability continues to bring about more vulnerability. Remember when I shared that my husband said I wasn't allowed to analyze his mom? Well, as we settled into more and more of a deeper groove, he was more inclined to share everything rather than the things he was supposed to say. His mom is a saint, so there hasn't been that much to uncover. But it demonstrates the willingness to take the armor off to reflect on where we've been so we know where we are headed. I really think that's everything. Maybe there are little scraps of information that my husband doesn't know about me and the same for me about him. But the more time we spend together, the more we both bloom together.

So having depth doesn't mean that we complain all the time. It also doesn't mean that we can ignore how our partner is feeling about the depth that we pursue. My husband will occasionally participate in psychoanalytic theory. But he also will say no when he's not feeling it. Fair. We need to show up for our partners when they are feeling wonky even if we believe they were in the wrong. It's not our job to judge, it is our job to support and validate.

Is depth correctable? Similar to a lot of answers I have given thus far, maybe. Because the lack of depth can be an ingrained part of someone's character in the same way it could be something that someone actually has control over. Try these things to sort through which one it is:

- Tell your partner what you need before you share the thing that dug up an aversive feeling. "Hey. I'm going to share this thing with you. The only thing I need from you is the validation of my experience."

- Prep them directly with the idea that you are craving a deeper dive into a particular issue. Ask them for consent before sharing. "Is now an okay time to share something complex with you?"

- Give the rough outline before sharing the details. "I need to talk about how I had a weird interaction with a family member. We both blew up. Now we aren't talking. Can I land this on you with a few more details?"

- Share a tangible love language need that they can do right now.

- Brainstorm a topic. Time each other while you're on an uninterrupted soapbox. The idea is that you have to keep talking about that one particular topic for a full five minutes.

Chapter 10

I want you to be BEDAZZLED

I always love it when people give me Cliffs Notes for different material, so I wanted to do the same for you. This is good stuff to have in your back pocket as you put yourself out there, as you try to see whether your current partnership will make it, or if you are already headed for something better. Keep me on your shoulder. What would dr_meaghan say? I'm incredibly picky, my expectations are probably way too high for a therapist, and the odds of me telling you that you could probably do better is pretty high.

I love all my clients, and I love you too. I want you to be **BEDAZZLED**. I want you to stop wasting your time and get into the kind of partnership that fuels your soul. I waited too long, nearly a decade, with the wrong partnership, and I now know what an incredible loss of my life years it was. Was it pointless? Definitely not. I took away a lot of valuable life lessons that now I get to share with you, but I think I could have had the same type of life lesson with half the time wasted. I don't know, the jury is still out.

Let's head back to **BECOMING**. When we find the best versions of ourselves and fully understand what we need and don't need, the best partners will land on us. Trying to figure yourself out after you've found a partner is substantially harder, and putting that kind of weight on a relationship has the capacity to tank it entirely.

Always work on how you **EXPRESS** yourself. We will never reach a time in life where we are allowed to kick back because we've reached perfection. If you think you're perfect, we should probably talk at some point. But for the rest of us, let's practice grace, patience, listening more, and speaking less. Let's work on our dispositions that cause us to express ourselves in certain ways that aren't entirely helpful.

Be **DELICATE** during conflict. Intimacy and fear can't exist in the same setting. Creating a culture of wholesomeness where both of us can rely on solutions in the distant future is the goal. Professing to end up aligned independent from how far we may feel will give both partners the chance to prove it.

How we present information is far more important than the details behind it.

Always stay **ACTIVE.** Our partners need our help because the organization you are creating depends on both of you. Don't get caught being the short end of the stick because one day your partner will resent the hell out of you and it will be hard to bring them back once you've lost them entirely.

Be **ZESTFUL** always. Find some sexual vigor. Start with emotional and physical intimacy and wrap it up with sex (or your own variation of sex that still meets physical needs). Flirt with your partner and never miss an opportunity to tell them how much they mean to you. How you couldn't live without them. Make them feel special because if you don't, somebody else will.

Have a **ZIPPY** way about you when it comes to giving something tangible to your partner. Your partner needs to carry your share of the weight to run a household. Pick an economic contribution and dive right in. Childcare, money, community involvement, handling a complex household, taking care of those who can't take care of themselves: all of these things will help.

Stay **LIKABLE**. Give something back to the world. Whether it be your sense of humor, incredible work ethic, your talent with a particular skill, or your willingness to just give extra time to others in need. If the world likes you and you're getting relatively decent feedback, there's a pretty good chance your partner will too.

Feel **EMPOWERED.** Nobody is going to love you in the way that you need if you don't think you're hot stuff. We love ourselves first and then we can offer love to others. Not in reverse order.

Activate your **DEPTH**. Feel deeply enough to give life a positive outlook. But not so deep that you're offending people or ignoring the read on their feelings. Put yourself in someone else's shoes and see their pain through their lens. It might shock you what you could find in those spaces.

Bring the **BEDAZZLED** in for the first time, dig it up in your current partnership, or start from scratch and find your way there. The transformation it has created in my own life is brag worthy, and I would love nothing more than to have you find the same thing in your own life and come to me bragging away. To have more partnerships in the world that people are bragging about couldn't possibly bring me more joy.

www.ingramcontent.com/pod-product-compliance
Lightning Source LLC
Chambersburg PA
CBHW050645160426
43194CB00010B/1822